Elvis in Hollywood

Recipes Fit for a King®

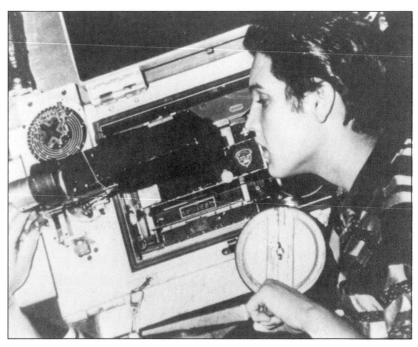

Elvis from the other side of the camera.

Elvis in Hollywood

Recipes Fit for a King®

Fit For A King® is a registered trademark owned by Elizabeth McKeon, Ralph Gevirtz, and Julie Bandy.

Photograph on back cover and text photgraphs are from the Linda Everett private collection. Pages 31 and 97 are from the Sandi Miller private collection. All rights reserved. Reprinted by permission.

Every effort has been made to locate current copyright holders of material reproduced or quoted in this book. Grateful acknowledgment is made for permission to reprint excerpts from the following:
Elvis A Biography by Jerry Hopkins © 1971 by Jerry Hopkins. Used by permission of Warner Books.
Elvis A Bio-Biography by Patsy Guy Hammondtree © 1985 by Patsy Guy Hammondtree. Used by permission of Greenwood Books.
Motion Picture and Television Magazine. August 1957; October 1957.
Saturday Evening Post. September 1965.

Published in Nashville, Tennessee, by Rutledge Hill Press, 211 Seventh Avenue North, Nashville, Tennessee 37219. Distributed in Canada by H. B. Fenn & Company, Ltd., Mississauga, Ontario L5S 1R7

Library of Congress Cataloging-in-Publication Data
McKeon, Elizabeth, 1962–
    Elvis in Hollywood : recipes fit for a king / Elizabeth McKeon.
        p.   cm.
    Includes index.
    ISBN 1-55853-301-X
    1. Presley, Elvis, 1935–1977. 2. Cookery, American. I. Title.
TX715.M474334 1994
641.5973—dc20   94-26883
                                                                          CIP

Printed in the United States of America
1 2 3 4 5 6 7 8 9—99 98 97 96 95 94

CONTENTS

An early publicity photo.

ELVIS PRESLEY

On April 1, 1956, Elvis Presley arrived in Hollywood. His first order of business was to make a screen test for producer Hal Wallis. Elvis read a scene from *The Rainmaker* opposite character actor Frank Faylen.

The screen test resulted in a three-film, seven-year contract with Wallis. Of that reading Wallis said, "Elvis in a very modern way had exactly the same power, virility, and sexual drive as Errol Flynn."

Elvis left Hollywood after the test, returning five months later to begin filming *Love Me Tender*, originally titled *The Reno Brothers*. Elvis was not given top billing, the only film in which he was not. The original film also did not include Elvis singing, but original songs were added later and the film was retitled *Love Me Tender*.

Elvis was so popular that when *Love Me Tender* premiered in New York in 1956 police were called in to control the crowds. Thousands mobbed the theater.

Elvis's next film, *Loving You*, released in 1957, was written especially for him. It also was the first film produced by Wallis for Paramount. In it Elvis plays Deke Rivers, a shy country boy who dreams of becoming a popular singer. The similarities between Elvis's life and his character's made critics question his acting ability, but fans weren't concerned about the plot. They were thrilled to see Elvis on the big screen.

With the release of *Jailhouse Rock* in 1957, critics became less critical of Elvis. Playing the character of Vince Everett, Elvis proved that he had what it took to become a serious actor.

In 1958 Paramount released *King Creole*, the second film produced by Wallis. It was Elvis's first film to be shot on location.

While working on *King Creole*, Elvis was called by Uncle Sam to serve in the army. Two years away from the motion picture industry had little effect on Elvis's fame and popularity. Producer

Hal Wallis saw Elvis's two-year stint in the army as an opportunity for creating another Presley film, *G.I. Blues*, his fifth.

After the success of *G.I. Blues*, Hollywood realized it had a problem: casting Elvis in just any film would prove to be difficult. After all, who would believe that any character Elvis portrayed was not really himself?

So Hollywood came up with a solution. They would cast their leading man with a pretty leading lady in a story with an uncomplicated plot, with a little rock 'n' roll thrown in for good measure. This proved to be a powerful formula.

From 1961 to 1969 Elvis made another twenty-six films, each using the same formula and each making a lot of money. Hal Wallis once said, "The only sure thing in show business is a Presley film."

Although Elvis once stated that he didn't care much for singing in his films, pointing out that his original screen test contained no singing, his dream of becoming an actor had come true.

"I was a powerful admirer of James Dean," Elvis once said. "I think he was one of the greatest actors I have ever seen. But I'm not going to try and copy anybody."

Elvis spent more than ten years of his life making thirty-one feature films and two documentaries. Some critics believe the work he produced in the fifties was his best. More than anything, however, he wanted to be known as a good actor dedicated to his craft.

He once said, "I'm trying to be myself in my acting, with my own name and my own style of acting."

FOREWORD

I first met Elvis on the Paramount Studio lot in Hollywood in 1965. I was there filming an episode of *Bonanza*, and Elvis was next door shooting a movie. He had heard I was there and sent one of his guys over. He said, "Elvis wants to meet you. He's a big fan of yours."

I went over to where Elvis was shooting, and we sat and talked. It was then I realized what a truly nice person he was and that we had a lot in common, such as our taste in music and our love of karate. We also shared the same taste in ladies. We discovered, much to our surprise, that we were dating the same girl. We both laughed, but I wonder if either of us meant it.

Before Elvis opened in Las Vegas, he came to see my show on a number of occasions. After the show, we would go to his or my suite and sit and swap lies, as guys will do. When you went to one of those parties, the girls usually stayed on one side of the room and the guys on the other. And that's where Elvis would be—with the guys, telling stories.

Elvis was very much a southern gentleman. We both were raised to respect women. He, like myself, would open doors for them and make sure nothing inappropriate or vulgar was said or done in front of them.

Aside from our friendship, Elvis and I had professional respect for one another. We frequently caught each other's shows. Sometimes he would walk out on stage at the beginning of his show and say, "Good evening, ladies and gentlemen, my name is Wayne Newton," and everyone would laugh. He truly had one calling in life, and that was to bring pleasure to the people who came to see him.

I always have been a big fan of his, and we were friends. In fact, in 1992 I released and co-wrote a song called "The Letter," which is about a letter Elvis wrote and then threw away during his final engagement at the Las Vegas Hilton. It went number one, and the video was voted video of the year on TNN.

My love and respect for Elvis as an entertainer, but more importantly as a friend, has been a beacon of light for me in a misty world. In retrospect, we realize Elvis was blessed with many talents, and one of the most admirable was his ability to recognize and utilize great talent around him.

No man's immortality can fade as long as those who loved him carry on his morals, principles, and standards of perfection and giving, and do so with all the loving qualities he exemplified. When history is written, it is sometimes neither just nor kind. For Elvis, however, history will be forced to admit that those who knew him and loved him have picked up the torch and marched on.

—Wayne Newton
Las Vegas, Nevada
January 1994

PREFACE

Elvis Presley arrived in Hollywood in 1956. As he was already established as The King of rock 'n' roll, motion pictures seemed the logical next step in his career. Elvis produced thirty-one feature films and two documentaries.

Elvis kept busy when he was in Hollywood. His life consisted of living in luxury hotels, dining in elegant restaurants, and visiting exclusive nightclubs where he frequently was spotted with his most recent leading lady.

While living in Hollywood Elvis made friends with such notable celebrities as Nick Adams, Natalie Wood, and Sal Mineo. On days away from the studio, he enjoyed riding his motorcycle above the hills of Bel Air or playing touch football at a nearby park. At other times he preferred the company of friends in his hotel suite. There they would watch television, listen to Elvis sing, or order from room service.

Elvis knew he was a long way from his home in Memphis and from the life he knew there. So he brought an entourage of family and friends with him. His ole boys, as they were known, worked for him twenty-four hours a day.

When Elvis went out on the town, his boys were to keep fans from getting too close to him. He often disguised himself so he could go out to a movie or a local eatery for a cheeseburger and Coke.

Here now is a collection of recipes popular during the time when Elvis was living in Hollywood. Some are foods he ate regularly, while others are for foods he served to his many guests. Follow him from the early days when he lived at the Knickerbockers Hotel, to lunches at the studio commissary, to driving up and down the Sunset Strip in his Cadillac. Elvis liked living in Hollywood, and here is a look at his life outside the studio gates.

—Elizabeth McKeon

Elvis Presley

INTRODUCTION

When I first went to work for Elvis Presley, he was living at 565 Perugia Way in Bel Air. He was twenty-eight years old and had just finished working on the movie Fun in Acapulco. In the six years that I worked for Elvis, he made eighteen movies, recorded I don't know how many songs, married, became a father, met the Beatles, taped his Singer television special, and had his first performances in Las Vegas.

In October of 1967 I went along with Elvis to Sedona, Arizona, where he was making Stay Away Joe. Elvis wanted me to cook home-style foods such as meat loaf and chicken for him and his boys.

I was Elvis's day cook, which meant that—among other things—I got to prepare his favorite meal of the day: breakfast. Sometimes he had me fix a hearty meal of eggs, bacon, biscuits, and gravy, and at other times he ate a simple meal of fruit and toast. Elvis ordered his meals daily, and every meal was different.

When I first came to cook for Elvis, I had heard that he didn't particularly care for chicken. So I went to the butcher and had a whole fryer cut up. I fried that up real good, and Elvis ate some. I put the leftovers in the refrigerator. Later I found two pieces missing and a trail of crumbs leading to Elvis's bedroom. Looking over the evidence, I said to him, "Well, that chicken didn't walk all by itself." From that time on, he loved chicken and ate it regularly.

When Elvis was living in Hollywood, fans would wait for him outside the house. Sometimes he would go out and visit with them, and other times he invited them in. He liked to sit and talk with them, and he even became good friends with some of them. Being the gracious host that he was, he would offer them refreshments. He also liked to throw small parties for his friends. He didn't drink alcohol, so there was always an assortment of soft drinks to go with the sandwiches and chips.

Every day was different when I worked for Elvis. I loved cooking for him and his family and friends. Because he liked home-style cooking, it was easy to prepare his meals. Even though I worked for him, Elvis always made me feel like I was a member of the family.

He was very generous, but the best gift was the house he bought for me so I would always have a place to live.

—Alvena Roy
July 1994
Los Angeles, California

Elvis's Star on the Hollywood Walk of Fame

FILMOGRAPHY

1956 *Love Me Tender*, 20th Century Fox. Producer: David Weisbart. Elvis Presley, Richard Egan, Debra Paget.

1957 *Loving You*, Paramount. Producer: Hal Wallis. Elvis Presley, Lizabeth Scott, Wendell Corey.

1957 *Jailhouse Rock*, MGM. Producer: Pandro Berman. Elvis Presley, Judy Tyler, Mickey Shaughessy.

1958 *King Creole*, Paramount. Producer: Hal Wallis. Elvis Presley, Carolyn Jones, Walter Matthau.

1960 *G.I. Blues*, Paramount. Producer: Hal Wallis. Elvis Presley, James Douglas, Juliet Prowse.

1960 *Flaming Star*, Paramount. Producer: David Weisbart. Elvis Presley, Steve Forrest, Barbara Eden.

1961 *Wild in the Country*, 20th Century Fox. Producer: Jerry Wald. Elvis Presley, Hope Lange, Tuesday Weld.

1961 *Blue Hawaii*, Paramount. Producer: Hal Wallis. Elvis Presley, Joan Blackman, Angela Lansbury.

1962 *Follow That Dream*, United Artists. Producer: David Weisbart. Elvis Presley, Arthur O'Connell, Ann Helm.

1962 *Kid Galahad*, United Artists. Producer: David Weisbart. Elvis Presley, Gig Young, Lola Albright, Ed Asner.

1962 *Girls! Girls! Girls!*, Paramount. Producer: Hal Wallis. Elvis Presley, Stella Stevens, Laurel Goodwin.

1963 *It Happened at the World's Fair*, MGM. Producer: Ted Richmond. Elvis Presley, Joan O'Brien, Gary Lockwood.

1963 *Fun in Acapulco*, Paramount. Producer: Hal Wallis. Elvis Presley, Ursula Andress, Elsa Cardenas.

1964 *Kissin' Cousins*, MGM. Producer: Sam Katzman. Elvis Presley, Arthur O'Connell, Jack Albertson, Yvonne Craig.

1964 *Viva Las Vegas*, MGM. Producer: Jack Cummings. Elvis Presley, Ann-Margret, William Demarest.

1964 *Roustabout*, Paramount. Producer: Hal Wallis. Elvis Presley, Barbara Stanwyck, Joan Freeman.

1965 *Girl Happy*, MGM. Producer: Joe Pasternak Elvis Presley, Shelley Fabares, Mary Ann Mobley, Gary Crosby.

1965 *Tickle Me*, Allied Artists. Producer: Ben Schwalb. Elvis Presley, Jocelyn Lane, Julie Adams.

1965 *Harum Scarum*, MGM. Producer: Sam Katzman. Elvis Presley, Mary Ann Mobley, Fran Jefferies.

1966 *Frankie and Johnny*, United Artists. Producer: Edward Small. Elvis Presley, Donna Douglas, Sue Ane Langdon.

1966 *Paradise, Hawaiian Style*, Paramount. Producer: Hal Wallis. Elvis Presley, Suzanne Leigh, James Shigeta.

1966 *Spinout*, MGM. Producer: Joe Pasternak. Elvis Presley, Shelley Fabares, Diane McBaine.

1967 *Easy Come, Easy Go*, Paramount. Producer: Hal Wallis. Elvis Presley, Pat Harrington, Dodie Marshall.

1967 *Double Trouble*, MGM. Producer: Judd Bernard. Elvis Presley, Annette Day, John Williams.

1967 *Clambake*, United Artists. Producer: Levy-Gardner. Elvis Presley, Shelley Fabares, Bill Bixby.

1968 *Stay Away Joe*, MGM. Producer: Douglas Lawrence. Elvis Presley, Burgess Meredith, Joan Blondell.

1968 *Speedway*, MGM. Producer: Douglas Lawrence. Elvis Presley, Nancy Sinatra, Bill Bixby.

1968 *Live a Little, Love a Little*, MGM. Producer: Douglas Lawrence. Elvis Presley, Michele Carey, Don Porter.

1969 *Charro*, National General Pictures. Producer: Charles Marquis Warren. Elvis Presley, Ina Balin, Victor French.

1969 *The Trouble with Girls*, MGM. Producer: Lester Welch. Elvis Presley, Marlyn Mason, Sheree North, Nichole Jaffe.

1970 *Change of Habit*, Universal. Producer: Joe Connelly. Elvis Presley, Mary Tyler Moore, Barbara McNair, Ed Asner.

1970 *Elvis, That's the Way It Is*, MGM. (Documentary)

1972 *Elvis on Tour*, MGM. (Documentary)

ACKNOWLEDGMENTS

I am grateful for the many people who assisted me with this project. Thanks to Linda Everett, for her friendship and for her endless hours spent researching photographs; my brother Michael, who made my travels to Hollywood a memorable adventure; Anne, who made sure I didn't work too hard; Jon, who helped me edit the manuscript; Dorothy, who supported me from the beginning; Harriet Stockanes and Carole Barrett; and Ralph Gevirtz and Julie Bandy.

Thanks also to Sandra Archer, Head Reference Librarian at the Margaret Herrick Library at the Academy of Motion Picture Arts and Sciences Library in Los Angeles, for her assistance with research; Gregg Stebben, who did the interviews with Elvis's co-stars; Elvis's co-stars: Mary Ann Mobley, Barbara Eden, Barbara McNair, Sheree North, Marlyn Mason, and Ed Asner, who took time from their busy schedules to share memories of their friend; Alvena Roy, who once again shared her memories of Elvis; and Wayne Newton, who shared fond memories of his friend.

Thanks to Stephen, Peggy, Bridget, Jack, Kathy, and John; my parents, who believed in this project from the start and supported me; my grandmother, Mildred, whose respect, friendship, and love I will always treasure; and Madeleine and Charlie, who kept me company while working on the manuscript.

Finally, thanks to Elvis himself, who shared his life with us all in such a generous and unselfish way.

Elvis in Hollywood

Recipes Fit for a King®

Love Me Tender *premiered in November 1956.*

*W*hen *Love Me Tender* was released to theaters nationwide, no less than 550 prints were ordered. At that time about 250 prints were ordered for most films. ■

MENUS

As with any cookbook, these menus are just suggestions. Vary the recipes that are in this book to create your own. These menuswere created from those dishes that Elvis especially enjoyed to eat.

FAVORITE PARTY SNACKS

Pepsi Cola
Celery Wheels
Bacon-Cheese Pastries
Cheddar Cheese Potato Chips
Party Mix
Corn Bread Sticks

ON THE TRAIN TO L.A.

Pepsi Cola
Bacon and Tomato Club Sandwich
Peanut Butter and Banana Sandwich

*E*lvis's star on the Hollywood Walk of Fame is located at 6777 Hollywood Boulevard. ∎

EARLY MORNING CALL

Coffee
Orange Juice
Hash Brown Potatoes
Scrambled Eggs with Bacon
Buttered Toast
Cantaloupe

Elvis driving in Bel Air.

AT THE ROADSIDE CAFÉ

Pepsi Cola
Fried Chicken
Mashed Potatoes and Gravy
Buttered Green Beans
Soda Biscuits

DINING AT THE DRIVE-IN

Pepsi Cola
Patty Melt
Cole Slaw
Onion Rings
Hot Fudge Sundae

ROOM SERVICE SUPPER

Pepsi Cola
Baked Pork Chops
Sauerkraut
Corn Spoon Bread
Tossed Green Salad
Orange Chiffon Cake

*E*lvis was said to be crazy about watermelon and cantaloupe. ■

PICNICS ON THE BEACH

Pepsi Cola
Cheeseburger
Baked Beans
Potato Salad
Strawberry Shortcake

BLUE PLATE SPECIAL

Coffee
Corn Chowder
Sloppy Joe Burger
Succotash
Boston Cream Pie

*W*hile filming, Elvis tended to follow a daily schedule. Although his activities varied, this was his basic itinerary when he was working in Hollywood:

6:00 A.M. Wake-up call from the studio.

7:00 A.M. Breakfast. Elvis loved sausage, bacon, and eggs.

8:00 A.M. Elvis arrives at the studio to practice his lines.

1:00 P.M. Lunch in his dressing room or at the studio commissary. A peanut-butter-and-banana sandwich was standard fare.

2:00 P.M. Cast and crew begin filming until 6:00 P.M.

7:00 P.M. Elvis memorizes his lines for the next day.

8:00 P.M. Dinner. Elvis preferred hamburgers and chocolate shakes.

9:00 P.M. Elvis and friends play pool, ride motorcycles, or watch a movie.

Elvis in his white Cadillac.

STUDIO COMMISSARY LUNCH

Coffee Mashed Potatoes and Gravy
Sauerkraut
Crisp Bacon
Biscuits
Fruit Gelatin with Whipped Cream

*B*ecause Elvis loved motorcycles, he refused to allow producer Hal Wallis to include a clause in any movie contract forbidding him to ride one. ■

LATE NIGHT SUPPER

Coffee
Baked Meat Loaf
Mixed Vegetables
White Bread
Chocolate Cake

THE SUNSET STRIP

Pepsi Cola
Chili Cheese Dogs
French Fries

*E*lvis didn't like foreign foods or small restaurants with too much atmosphere. He preferred dinner to be a fast-food snack at the local drive-in before going to the Ocean Park Pier. ■

BIRTHDAYS IN HOLLYWOOD
Milk
Pork Roast
Creamed Potatoes
Mixed Vegetables
Corn Spoon Bread
Banana Pudding

LUNCH AMONG THE STARS
Pepsi Cola
Steak
Tossed Green Salad
Pan-Fried Potatoes
Bread with Butter
Apple Pie

*E*lvis liked to nibble on peanuts and popcorn while on the movie set. ■

ON THE TOWN
Pepsi Cola
Grilled Ham and Cheese Sandwich
Cheddar Cheese Potato Chips
Lemon Coconut Cake

WEEKEND BRUNCH
Coffee
Eggs Benedict
Corn Beef Hash
Pan-Fried Potatoes
Fruit Salad

*E*lvis's first appearance in Hollywood was in October 1957. He played for two nights at the Pan-Pacific Auditorium, 7600 Beverly Boulevard. The crowd of 9,000 included such notable celebrities as Natalie Wood, Nick Adams, and Sammy Davis, Jr. After the show, Elvis invited his friends to his emerald green suite at the Beverly Wilshire Hotel. He offered them plenty of cheeseburgers, Cokes, and chocolate cake. ■

Elvis at a party with friends.

*R*ecord producer Bones Howe has memories of Elvis in Hollywood.

"Elvis and his boys would come to town and take an entire floor at the Roosevelt Hotel on Hollywood Boulevard or at the Plaza near Hollywood and Vine, and later the Knickerbocker Hotel on Ivar, just north of Hollywood Boulevard. They had to take the whole floor because they couldn't guard his room otherwise. Girls would crawl up the fire escape, and Elvis would encourage them.

"They came to Hollywood traveling in one of those Cadillacs with an extra section in the middle. From the time they got up in the morning, they'd drive up and down Hollywood Boulevard. They would pull up to a stop light, and just before the light changed—if there were girls standing on the corner—Elvis would roll the window down, take his sunglasses off, and say hello. And then the light would change and they'd take off, leaving hundreds of people wandering around the intersection screaming and jumping up and down and chasing the Cadillac down the street. Elvis just loved it.

"Afternoons were spent in the large funky room that was Studio B at Radio Recorders at 7000 Santa Monica Boulevard, a few blocks from Hollywood High School. For Elvis, the room was booked by the week, not by the hour." ■

A lucky fan gets Elvis's autograph.

APPETIZERS

Bacon-Cheese Pastries

¾ cup shortening
2¼ cups all-purpose flour
1 teaspoon salt

⅓ cup cold water
4 slices bacon
¼ pound Cheddar cheese

In a medium bowl combine the shortening, flour, and salt with a pastry blender. Add the cold water a little at a time. Stir with a fork until portions of the dough are moist. Roll the dough into a ball. Wrap in waxed paper and refrigerate for 15 minutes.

Turn the dough onto a lightly floured board and roll to ⅛-inch thickness, rolling from the center toward the edges. Cut into 2-inch squares and mark each with a diagonal line.

In a skillet fry the bacon until crisp. Drain on paper towels. Crumble the bacon. Grate the cheese and mix it with the bacon. Place a teaspoon of filling onto half of each pastry. Fold over diagonally and press the edges firmly together. Bake at 400° for 10 minutes or until golden brown.

Makes 4 servings.

*O*n his first Saturday night in Hollywood, Elvis was spotted at an amusement park on Long Beach, where a crowd gathered to watch him win several stuffed Teddy Bears at one of the game booths. Oddly enough, when he returned to the Knickerbockers Hotel, he didn't have any of the bears he had won. ∎

Meatballs

1 tablespoon butter	½ cup bread crumbs
2 tablespoons minced onion	½ cup light cream
½ pound ground beef	1 egg
¼ pound ground veal	½ teaspoon salt
¼ pound ground pork	Ground allspice

In a skillet melt the butter and sauté the minced onion until transparent. In a medium bowl blend together the ground beef, veal, and pork. Add the sautéed onion and bread crumbs. Mix in the cream, egg, salt, and allspice to taste. Blend thoroughly.

Using a teaspoon mound the mixture into smooth balls. Brown in the same skillet used to sauté the onions. Brown evenly by shaking the skillet as the meat is cooking. Once browned, reduce the heat and simmer about 15 minutes or until done.

Makes 5 dozen.

*R*estaurants Elvis preferred in Los Angeles:

Chasen's
9039 Beverly Boulevard
It is said that Elvis liked the prime rib.

Hamburger Hamlet
Sunset Boulevard

Formosa Café
7156 Santa Monica Boulevard
According to legend, Elvis once gave
a white Cadillac Eldorado convertible to a waitress
named Dora at the Formosa. She proudly displayed the vehicle
on the front lawn of her Melrose Avenue home.

Tiny Naylor's
La Cienega at Wilshire Boulevard
Elvis would stop in for a quick cheeseburger and Coke. ■

Elvis relaxing in his hotel suite.

*H*otels Elvis stayed in while in Los Angeles:

Hollywood Knickerbocker Hotel
1714 North Ivar Avenue

Roosevelt Hotel
7000 Hollywood Boulevard

Regent Beverly Wilshire
9500 Wilshire Boulevard ■

Hamburger Puffs

1 cup water	¼ pound ground beef
½ cup butter	1 small onion, chopped
¾ teaspoon salt	1 green bell pepper, chopped
1 cup all-purpose flour, sifted	Salt and pepper to taste
4 eggs	

In a saucepan boil the water. Add the butter and salt. Reduce the heat and add the flour. Stir with a wooden spoon until the mixture forms a ball and leaves the sides of the saucepan. Beat in the eggs, one at a time. Continue beating until the mixture is smooth.

With a teaspoon drop the dough about 2 inches apart on a greased baking sheet. Bake at 400° for 45 minutes or until golden. Let the puffs cool on a rack.

In a skillet brown the ground beef with the onion and green pepper. Drain. Season with salt and pepper. Split each pastry puff and fill with the hamburger mixture.

Makes 1 dozen.

Cheese Puffs

½ cup butter, softened	½ teaspoon Worcestershire
2 cups grated Cheddar cheese	sauce
Cayenne pepper to taste	1 cup all-purpose flour

In a medium bowl blend together the butter, cheese, and seasonings. Add the flour and blend thoroughly. Wrap the mixture in waxed paper and refrigerate until chilled.

Roll the dough into walnut-size balls. Place the balls 2 inches apart on an ungreased baking sheet. Bake at 350° for 15 minutes.

Makes 2 dozen.

Elvis and Nick Adams

*E*lvis's long-time friend Nick Adams said that the King was one of the most likeable guys in Hollywood. The reason for his popularity, Adams said, was "because Elvis is real, and he is lots of fun." ■

Crullers

3½ cups all-purpose flour
4 teaspoons baking powder
1 teaspoon salt
½ teaspoon ground cinnamon
¼ teaspoon grated nutmeg
1 cup sugar

¼ cup butter
2 eggs, well beaten
1 cup milk
Confectioners' sugar
Oil

In a medium bowl sift together the flour, baking powder, salt, cinnamon, and nutmeg. In a separate bowl cream together the sugar and butter. Add the eggs and beat until light and fluffy. Add the flour mixture alternately with the milk. Add a little more flour if needed to make a soft dough. Turn the dough onto a floured board. Roll to ¼-inch thickness and cut with a floured doughnut cutter.

Fry in hot oil for 2 minutes on each side or until lightly browned. Drain on paper towels. Dust with confectioners' sugar.

Makes 40.

Vegetable Fritters

1 small eggplant
Salt
1 large zucchini
½ small cauliflower

¾ cup all-purpose flour
2 eggs
¼ cup milk
Oil

Slice the eggplant thinly. Place the slices in a colander and sprinkle with salt. Cover and set aside. Slice the zucchini and divide the cauliflower into florets and set aside.

In a mixing bowl sift the flour with a pinch of salt. Make a well in the center. Add the eggs to the well and mix them into the flour. Gradually add the milk and beat until the batter is smooth. Rinse the eggplant and pat it dry with paper towels. Dip the vegetables into the batter. Fry in hot oil for 30 seconds on each side or until golden. Drain and serve.

Makes 6 servings.

Elvis at his screen test for Love Me Tender.

*W*hile filming *Love Me Tender*, at the end of each day's shooting the cast went to Richard Egan's dressing room for cocktails. Elvis didn't boycott these soirées, but he declined any hard liquor. Instead, he would drink a Coke or a 7-Up. He did, however, have a passion for the hors d'oeuvres. He'd come in every afternoon and ask cheerfully, "Where are all the goodies?" ∎

Celery Wheels

1 4½-ounce can deviled ham	1 teaspoon Worcestershire sauce
1 3-ounce package cream cheese	1 tablespoon sour cream
6 stuffed green olives, minced	12 celery sticks

In a small bowl blend the deviled ham with the cream cheese. Add the minced olives, Worcestershire sauce, and sour cream, and blend until smooth and creamy. Trim the leaves from the celery sticks and clean the celery thoroughly. Pat dry with paper towels.

Fill each celery stick with the ham mixture. Press 2 filled sticks together. Wrap tightly in plastic wrap. Refrigerate for 4 hours.

When ready to serve remove the plastic wrap. With a sharp knife cut the sticks into slices about ½-inch thick.

Makes 2 dozen.

When Elvis first came to Hollywood, he lived behind electrically operated gates in a modern villa in Bel Air. Inside, the place looked more like a rec hall than a home. It was filled with pinball machines, a pool table, shelves of books and stuffed animals, hi-fi's, radios, soft-drink-only bars, and round ski-lodge fireplaces.

Elvis did not touch liquor, and he smoked only an occasional cigar. He attempted to keep in shape by dieting on yogurt and coffee, but now and then he succumbed to temptation. One lunch consisted of a bowl of gravy, a bowl of mashed potatoes, nine slices of bacon, a quart of milk, a lettuce salad, tomato juice, and six slices of bread.

Once Elvis said, "I took the Rolls out for a drive, but the freeways were so crowded that I came back and watched TV."

He spent weekends in a Beverly Hills park playing football with other Hollywood stars. Pat Boone and Lee Majors were among the grunt-and-groaners. This time no one kept Elvis off the first string. The team garb was red jerseys, white helmets, and blue sweat pants: the "Patriotic Presleys." Enough to make the Colonel proud.

The crowd was equally colorful. Mostly they were young ladies in beehive coiffures, tight capri pants, and too much make-up. After the game, a chosen few would be invited to the house. Invitations were priceless and nontransferable. Those passed over on the initial inspection would play anyway and stand outside for hours, hoping a few replacements might be needed. ■

*H*omes Elvis lived in while working in Hollywood:

In 1960 he moved to 565 Perguia Way. Among his neighbors were Pat Boone and Greer Garson.

In 1963 he moved to 1059 Bellagio Road in Bel Air. Some of its most impressive features were a huge marble entrance, a large tennis court, and a bowling alley in the basement.

In 1964 Elvis moved to 100550 Rocca Place in Stone Canyon near the Bel Air Hotel.

In 1965 Elvis bought 1174 Hillcrest Road in the exclusive Trusdale Estates. It had four large bedrooms and six bathrooms. The backyard contained an Olympic-size swimming pool.

In 1967 Elvis moved to 144 Monovale Road. He installed a soda fountain and a pool table there. ■

1174 Hillcrest Road

144 Monovale Road

An early publicity photo

*W*hile filming *Love Me Tender*, Elvis lived at the Knickerbocker Hotel on Ivar Avenue. Hotel switchboard operators logged 237 phone messages for Elvis on his first day there. ■

Pickled Eggs

12 hard-boiled eggs
2 cups cider vinegar
2 tablespoons sugar
1 teaspoon salt

1 teaspoon spice made from:
  3 peppercorns, 1 clove garlic,
  celery seed, ginger root
1 small peeled onion

Place the peeled eggs in a mixing bowl and set them aside.

In a saucepan combine the cider vinegar, sugar, salt, spices, and onion. Bring the mixture to a boil. Reduce the heat and simmer for 8 minutes. Pour the mixture over the eggs.

Cover the bowl and marinate the eggs overnight in the refrigerator. Drain before serving. Cut the eggs in half and arrange them on a platter of shredded lettuce.

Makes 2 dozen servings.

In 1957 Nudie's, the Hollywood costume firm, made Elvis's gold lame tuxedo at a cost of $10,000. ■

Deviled Ham Snacks

¼ cup melted butter
1 cup sour cream
1 egg
1 teaspoon baking powder
½ teaspoon salt

2¼ cups all-purpose flour
1 4½-ounce can deviled ham
¼ cup chopped mushrooms
¼ cup chopped celery
Tabasco to taste

In a medium bowl combine the butter, sour cream, egg, baking powder, salt, and flour. Blend thoroughly. Turn the dough onto a floured board. Roll out the dough and cut it into triangles about 3 inches in size. Pinch the dough upwards at the three points. Place on a baking sheet. Prick each with a fork. Bake at 425° for 15 minutes or until golden brown.

In a small bowl blend the deviled ham, mushrooms, and celery. Season with Tabasco sauce. Remove the pastries from the oven. Fill each pastry with the deviled ham mixture. Return the pastries to the oven and continue baking until the mixture is hot.

Makes 12 servings.

Dill Pickles

3 pounds medium-size cucumbers   1 cup vinegar
6 stalks fresh dill   ½ cup salt
6 green grape leaves   4 cups water

Wash and sterilize 3 1-quart jars and lids in boiling water. Set aside.

Wash the cucumbers in cold water. Pack them vertically in the sterilized quart jars. Leave enough space in the top of each jar for the dill and grape leaves. Place some of the dill in between the cucumbers and some on top. Place grape leaves in the same manner.

In a saucepan heat the vinegar, salt, and water just to boiling. Immediately pour the brine over the cucumbers to about ¼ inch from the top. Seal and store in a cool dark place. The cucumbers will pickle in about 3 to 4 weeks.

Makes 3 quarts.

Enjoying a party with friends.

Party Mix

⅓ cup butter
¼ cup steak sauce
2 teaspoons seasoned salt
2 cups shredded corn cereal

2 cups shredded rice cereal
2 cups shredded wheat cereal
1 cup cashews

In a saucepan melt the butter over low heat. Mix in the steak sauce and seasoned salt. Add the cereal and cashews. Blend until all the pieces are coated in butter.

Place the saucepan in the oven. Bake at 250° for 1 hour. Stir the mixture every 15 minutes. To serve, remove the party mix from the saucepan and spread on waxed paper. Cool.

Makes 7 cups.

*I*f the original titles for some of Elvis's films were changed, his screen credits would be altogether different.

The Reno Brothers became *Love Me Tender*
Running Wild became *Loving You*
Café Europa became *G.I. Blues*
Flaming Lance became *Flaming Star*
Hawaii Beach Boy became *Blue Hawaii*
Pioneer Go Home became *Follow That Dream*
Welcome Aboard became *Girls! Girls! Girls!*
Mister, Will You Marry Me? became
It Happened at the World's Fair
Vacation in Acapulco became *Fun in Acapulco*
Right This Way Folks became *Roustabout*
Harum Holiday became *Harum Scarum*
Polynesian Paradise became *Paradise Hawaiian Style*
Always at Midnight became *Spinout*
Port of Call became *Easy Come, Easy Go*
You're Killing Me became *Double Trouble*
Too Big for Texas became *Clambake*
Born Rich became *Stay Away Joe*
Pot Luck became *Speedway*
Come Hell, Come Sundown became *Charro* ■

Appetizer Burgers

10 slices white bread	1 tablespoon Worcestershire
Butter	sauce
1 pound ground beef	½ teaspoon salt
1 tablespoon minced onion	¼ cup chili sauce

Toast the bread on one side. Butter the untoasted side of the bread. Cut each slice into four equal portions about 1½ inches.

In a mixing bowl combine the ground beef, onion, Worcestershire sauce, and salt. Shape into 40 balls. Place a ball on the buttered side of each piece of bread and flatten somewhat. Make a well in the center of the meat mixture. Broil for 5 minutes or until the meat is cooked and the edges of the bread are toasted. Before serving fill the wells with the chili sauce.

Makes 40.

Ham Pancakes

1 cup pancake mix	2 tablespoons mayonnaise
¼ cup cornmeal	2 tablespoons cream cheese,
1½ cups milk	softened
1 egg, beaten	1 teaspoon horseradish
1 tablespoon butter, melted	2 cups cooked ham, chopped

In a mixing bowl combine the pancake mix with the cornmeal. Blend in the milk, egg, and butter. Pour 1 tablespoon of batter at a time onto a hot, greased griddle. Fry for 2 minutes on each side.

In a mixing bowl blend the mayonnaise with the cream cheese. Mix in the horseradish and blend thoroughly. Add the chopped ham. Spoon a little of the ham mixture on top of each pancake. Roll and fasten with wooden toothpicks. Arrange the rolls on a baking sheet. Place under a hot broiler and heat an additional 2 minutes.

Makes 2 dozen.

Cheddar Cheese Potato Chips

1 8-ounce bag regular potato chips
1 cup grated Cheddar cheese

½ teaspoon leaf thyme
¼ cup diced black olives, drained

Evenly spread the potato chips onto an ungreased baking sheet. Crumble the grated cheese over the chips. Sprinkle the olives and thyme over the cheese. Bake at 350° for 5 minutes or until the cheese has melted. Serve hot.

Serves 4.

*E*lvis's father, Vernon, had a nonspeaking part in *Live a Little, Love a Little*. His mother, Gladys, and Vernon appeared as audience members in *Loving You*. ■

Richard Egan and Debra Paget present Elvis
with a Teddy Bear.

Elvis greeting fans.

When Elvis stayed at the Knickerbocker Hotel, a fan club calling themselves the "Hotel Hounds" kept a steady vigil at his doorstep. It was not easy to become a member. One had to have been kissed by Elvis and had to be able to sing "Heartbreak Hotel" backwards. ■

Elvis getting a few pointers on his dancing.

Appetizer Frankfurters

½ cup soy sauce
1 tablespoon sugar
1 teaspoon minced onion

½ teaspoon ground ginger
¾ pound cocktail frankfurters

In a large shallow bowl blend the soy sauce, sugar, onion, and ginger. Add the frankfurters and marinate them for 2 hours. Bake at 350° for 15 minutes. Drain and serve while still warm.

Makes 1 dozen.

*B*arbara Eden co-starred opposite Elvis in *Flaming Star* in 1960. She tells about working with Elvis.

What was your first impression of Elvis when you met him?
"My first impression of Elvis was that he was a regular guy. I wasn't nervous about meeting him. I was on edge, but it was a good feeling because you don't know how the chemistry will work. He was a very nice man, a very polite southern gentleman."

What was it like on the set working with him?
"He had a lot of his 'cousins' around him. At that time, I believed they were all his cousins, but they weren't, of course. They were his buddies. They were there with their guitars, and they played music and sang songs between shots. Elvis's father was there a lot. And, of course, Colonel Parker who was selling pictures and stuff. He had a little place set up on the sound stage with pictures and records of Elvis. I don't know if anyone bought them, but they were there."

Do you remember eating with Elvis on the set?
"I remember eating with Elvis because we were on location and he would eat what we all ate. We talked about diet and food because he watched his weight at the time. He knew his face could get round. He said, 'I just have to watch it because my cheeks get puffy. Unfortunately, I like southern cooking.' "

What other things would you both talk about?
"He was concerned about the film because it was the first time he played a straight part and he didn't sing a song. Incidentally, it didn't sell tickets, and so they brought us all back in and he sang a song. He got wonderful reviews for the movie. He did a fabulous acting job. He talked about acting, and he was good. He liked acting. I will always treasure that memory and the film and how good an actor he was."

Do you have a fond memory of the time you spent with Elvis?
"I was nineteen years old then, and my sister was still at home. She was twelve, and she called me every night, 'Please, please, please get me his autograph! Please get me his picture!' You don't do that when you are working with someone. Finally, though, Elvis gave me a picture. 'To Allison,' he wrote. 'Well, I'll just have to wait until you grow up since your sister is married already.' It was very sweet." ■

BEVERAGES

Spiced Iced Tea

4 cups strong hot tea
Grated lemon rind
Grated orange rind
½ cup sugar

½ teaspoon whole cloves
1 cinnamon stick
½ cup water

Make tea double strength. Grate the lemon and orange rind using the whole fruit. In a saucepan mix the lemon rind, orange rind, sugar, cloves, and cinnamon stick. Pour in the water. Bring the mixture to a boil, reduce the heat, and simmer about 5 minutes. Strain and add to the tea. Refrigerate until well chilled.

Makes 1 quart.

*E*lvis liked a personal, homelike atmosphere wherever he was. ∎

Pineapple Mint Julep

Fresh mint
¾ cup sugar
¾ cup fresh lemon juice

3 cups pineapple juice
3 cups ginger ale

Wash the mint leaves. Drain. In a small bowl cover the mint with the sugar. Add the lemon juice. Set aside for 15 minutes.

Add the pineapple juice. Pour the mixture into a pitcher filled with crushed ice. Add the ginger ale. Garnish with mint.

Makes 8 servings.

Minted Tea Lemonade

2 tablespoons mint jelly
4 cups hot tea

1 6-ounce can frozen lemonade
concentrate

Dissolve the mint jelly in the hot tea. Mix in the lemonade. Refrigerate until thoroughly chilled.

Makes 4 servings.

Spiced Pineapple Punch

1 cup sugar
1½ cups water
2 cinnamon sticks
8 whole cloves

4 cups pineapple juice
½ cup fresh lemon juice
1 cup orange juice

In a saucepan combine the sugar, water, cinnamon sticks, and cloves. Simmer over low heat for 3 minutes. Strain. Add the pineapple juice, lemon juice, and orange juice. Pour the punch into a pitcher filled with crushed ice.

Makes 8 servings.

Spicy Fruit Punch

2½ cups grapefruit juice
2½ cups pineapple juice
⅓ cup sugar

2 cinnamon sticks
1 teaspoon whole cloves

In a saucepan combine the grapefruit juice and pineapple juice.
Add the sugar, cinnamon sticks, and cloves, and heat to boiling. Reduce the heat and simmer for 5 minutes. Strain. Serve hot.
Makes 8 servings.

Cranberry Cooler

2 1-pint bottles cranberry juice
cocktail
¼ cup fresh lemon juice

Crushed ice
4 cups orange sherbet
Mint

In a chilled pitcher blend the cranberry juice and lemon juice. Fill
8 tall glasses with crushed ice. Pour the juice over the ice, filling
glasses about ¾ full. Place a scoop of orange sherbet on top of each
serving. Garnish with mint.
Makes 8 servings.

*A*mong Elvis's favorite foods were eggs (fried hard on both
sides) pork chops, and fruit. For a midnight snack he liked
peanut-butter-and-banana sandwiches on white bread with a cold
glass of milk or Pepsi. ■

Fruit Fizz

1 egg white
¾ cup sugar
Ground ginger
Ground allspice

½ cup fresh lemon juice
1 cup orange juice
4 cups carbonated water

Beat the egg white until foamy. Add the sugar and a pinch of ginger
and allspice. Beat until stiff. Add the lemon juice and orange juice.
Mix well. Add the carbonated water. Serve in tall glasses filled
with ice cubes.
Makes 6 servings.

Elvis with co-star Nancy Sinatra.

*A*ccording to Mary Jenkins, who worked for Elvis as one of his cooks, his favorite snack was a "smooth peanut-butter-and-banana sandwich fried in lots of butter. For breakfast he liked pork sausage wrapped in biscuits that were fried." ■

Grape Juice Cocktail

1½ tablespoons sugar
1½ tablespoons water
6 tablespoons orange juice

½ cup grape juice
½ cup carbonated water
Crushed ice

In a beverage shaker mix the sugar and water. Add the orange juice, grape juice, and carbonated water. Blend until well mixed. Place crushed ice in 4 tall glasses. Pour the cocktail over the ice.
Makes 4 servings.

Orangeade

1 cup sugar	¼ cup fresh lemon juice
1 cup water	2 cups orange juice
Rind of 2 lemons grated	4 cups water

In a saucepan combine the sugar, 1 cup water, and lemon rind. Stir over low heat until the sugar has dissolved. Bring the syrup to a boil. Cook for 7 minutes. Cool thoroughly. Add the lemon juice, orange juice, and 4 cups of water. Pour into a pitcher filled with crushed ice.

Makes 6 servings.

Iced Mocha

6 tablespoons chocolate syrup	3 cups cold milk
3 cups strong coffee	Vanilla ice cream
Sugar	Whipped cream

In a medium bowl blend the chocolate syrup with the coffee. Add sugar to taste. Refrigerate until thoroughly chilled. In a pitcher combine the coffee mixture and milk. Pour into tall glasses. Add a spoonful of vanilla ice cream to each serving. Top with whipped cream.

Makes 6 servings.

Iced Coffee Frappé

2 eggs, beaten	3 cups strong coffee
Pinch of salt	1 cup cold milk
¾ cup sugar	½ cup heavy cream

In the top of a double boiler over simmering water blend the eggs, salt, sugar, coffee, and milk. Cook the mixture until it sticks to a spoon, stirring constantly. Refrigerate until thoroughly chilled.

Before serving fold in the whipped cream. Pour into tall glasses filled with crushed ice.

Makes 6 servings.

Another publicity photo

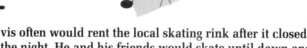

*E*vis often would rent the local skating rink after it closed for the night. He and his friends would skate until dawn and eat plenty of hot dogs and drink plenty of Pepsi. ■

Black Raspberry Soda

2 tablespoons seedless raspberry   ½ cup ginger ale
    jam   Vanilla ice cream
Salt   1 teaspoon cream

In a tall glass combine the raspberry jam, a pinch of salt, the cream, and ¼ cup of ginger ale. Stir to blend. Add a scoop of vanilla ice cream and the remaining ginger ale.
    Makes 1 serving.

Cherry Soda

2 tablespoons chopped
   maraschino cherries
1 tablespoon maraschino juice

1 teaspoon cream
Vanilla ice cream
Ginger ale

In a tall glass combine the chopped cherries and maraschino juice. Add the cream and ginger ale. Stir. Add the ice cream and ¼ cup of ginger ale. Stir to mix thoroughly.
   Makes 1 serving.

*E*lvis liked living in Hollywood. He always had his guys around for practical jokes and good fun. And the studio gave him a secretary for running his errands. ■

Signing autographs on the set of Live a Little, Love a Little.

Raspberry Soda

2 tablespoons frozen raspberries   **1 scoop vanilla ice cream**
Carbonated water

Place the partially thawed raspberries in a tall glass. Fill ¾ full with
cold carbonated water. Add the ice cream.
   Makes 1 serving.

Elvis in front of the gates at his Hillcrest house.

Pulling into his Hillcrest house.

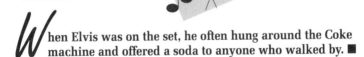

*W*hen Elvis was on the set, he often hung around the Coke machine and offered a soda to anyone who walked by. ■

Banana Shake

1 banana puréed
1 cup cold milk
1 teaspoon sugar
⅓ cup orange juice

1 large scoop vanilla ice cream
Pinch of salt
Whipped cream

In a blender combine the puréed banana with the milk and orange juice. Add ice cream, sugar, and salt. Blend until frothy. Do not overblend. Pour into a tall glass. Top with whipped cream.

Makes 1 serving.

Banana-Chocolate Shake

1 ripe banana
1 cup cold milk
2 tablespoons chocolate syrup

1 large scoop vanilla ice cream
1 teaspoon sugar

Peel and slice the banana. Mash with a fork until smooth. In a blender combine the banana, milk, chocolate syrup, ice cream, and sugar. Blend well to mix all ingredients. Serve cold.
Makes 1 serving.

Cherry Shake

1 cup cherry pie filling
2 cups vanilla ice cream
2 cups milk

2 tablespoons fresh lemon juice
Cherry ice cream

In a blender combine the cherry pie filling, vanilla ice cream, milk, and lemon juice. Mix until smooth. If too thick add more milk.
To serve place a scoop of cherry ice cream in a tall glass. Pour the cherry mixture over the ice cream.
Makes 4 servings.

Chocolate Mint Shake

2 tablespoons chocolate syrup
1 cup cold milk
1 scoop vanilla ice cream

2 drops peppermint extract
Whipped cream

In a blender combine the chocolate syrup, milk, and ice cream. Blend until thoroughly mixed. Add the peppermint extract and blend for 20 seconds. Pour into a tall glass. Top with whipped cream.
Makes 1 serving.

Elvis in a publicity photo.

*E*lvis's hold on women was the product of a high-pitched combination of the mystery of matinee idol, the challenge of a man of spirit and adventure who breaks with tradition, plus the sheer magnetism of a young man with a come-hither look that spelled defiance and romance all at once. ■

Orange Shake

½ cup orange juice
1 cup cold milk
¼ teaspoon almond extract

1 scoop vanilla ice cream
Sugar to taste
Whipped cream

In a blender combine the orange juice, milk, and ice cream. Blend until frothy. Add the almond extract and sugar to taste. Pour into a tall glass. Top with whipped cream.
    Makes 1 serving.

Pineapple Shake

1 small can crushed pineapple
1 cup cold milk
1 scoop vanilla ice cream

Whipped cream
Sugar to taste

In a blender combine the pineapple, milk, and ice cream. Blend until frothy. Add sugar to taste. Pour into a tall glass. Top with whipped cream.
Makes 1 serving.

Strawberry Shake

½ cup crushed strawberries
1 cup cold milk
1 scoop vanilla ice cream

Sugar
Whipped cream

In a blender combine the crushed strawberries, milk, and ice cream. Blend until frothy. Add sugar to taste. Pour into a tall glass. Top with whipped cream.
Makes 1 serving.

*E*lvis preferred his eggs covered in black pepper. They were always served with King Cotton bacon, which he had flown to the West Coast while he was living in Hollywood. ■

Chocolate Malted Milk

3 tablespoons chocolate syrup
3 teaspoons malted milk powder
1 scoop vanilla ice cream

1 cup cold milk
Whipped cream

In a shaker combine the chocolate syrup with the malted milk. Shake until well blended. Add the vanilla ice cream and milk. Shake thoroughly. Pour into a tall glass. Top with whipped cream.
Makes 1 serving.

Elvis wanted to be known for his own style of acting.

*E*lvis liked to drink his coffee very hot with a splash of cream and a teaspoon of sugar. ■

Coffee Malted Milk

3 tablespoons coffee
3 teaspoons malted milk powder
1 scoop vanilla ice cream

1 cup cold milk
Whipped cream

In a shaker combine the coffee with the malted milk. Shake until well blended. Add the ice cream and milk. Shake thoroughly. Pour into a tall glass. Top with whipped cream.

Makes 1 serving.

Elvis dancing with Ann-Margret in Viva Las Vegas.

*A*nn-Margret reminisced, "When I like someone I say, `Scoobie.' Elvis is scoobie." ■

Chocolate Eggnog

3 tablespoons chocolate syrup   Salt
1 cup cold milk   1 tablespoon sugar
1 egg, separated

In a blender mix the chocolate syrup and milk. Add the egg yolk and salt to taste. Blend until thoroughly mixed. Beat the egg white until foamy and add the sugar.

To serve pour the chocolate mixture into a tall glass and top with the egg white.

Makes 1 serving.

Elvis Presley

*H*ollywood didn't change Elvis Presley one bit. The matinee idol remained a shy country boy. He preferred simple get-togethers with friends to glamorous parties, a cheeseburger at a local drive-in instead of a steak dinner at a fancy restaurant. For fun, he enjoyed riding motorcycles and going to amusement parks. He liked the feel of flashy clothes and high-priced jewelry. There probably wasn't anything he wouldn't have done for a friend, and probably nothing he didn't. ■

Elvis with Barbara Eden on the set of Flaming Star.

SOUPS AND SALADS

Corn Chowder

6 large soda crackers
2 cups milk
3 slices salt pork
1 medium onion, sliced
4 medium potatoes, sliced

2 cups water
2 cups whole kernel corn,
  cooked
Salt and pepper to taste

In a small mixing bowl soak the soda crackers in the milk. Set the bowl aside.

Cut the salt pork into small cubes. In a large saucepan cook the pork with the onion until tender and somewhat brown. Add the sliced potatoes and water. Continue cooking until the potatoes are done. Add the corn and cracker mixture. Season with salt and pepper, and bring the chowder to a boil.

Makes 4 servings.

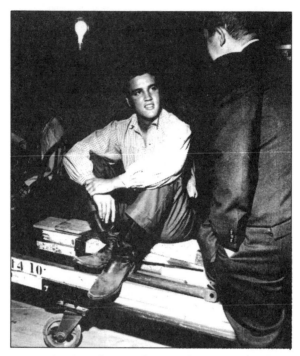

Interviewing Elvis on the set of Love Me Tender.

Hamburger & Vegetable Soup

½ pound ground beef
1 large onion, chopped
1 clove garlic, minced
½ cup chopped celery
3 carrots, chopped
½ cup diced green beans

2 medium potatoes, peeled and diced
1 tablespoon all-purpose flour
6 cups boiling water
1 teaspoon salt
Pepper to taste
Cayenne pepper to taste

In a soup pot brown the ground beef. Drain all but 1 tablespoon of fat. Add the chopped onion and minced garlic, and cook until the onion is transparent, but not brown. Add the celery, carrots, green beans, and potatoes. Continue cooking, stirring frequently, for 3 minutes. Add the flour and boiling water, and season with salt, pepper, and cayenne pepper. Simmer for 20 minutes or until all the vegetables are soft and thoroughly cooked.

Makes 4 servings.

Bacon & Potato Soup

6 slices bacon
3 small white onions, chopped
4 green onions, chopped
2 tablespoons all-purpose flour
6 cups beef bouillon
4 potatoes, sliced thinly

½ cup sour cream, room
  temperature
½ cup light cream
2 egg yolks
1 tablespoon minced parsley

In a soup pot fry the bacon until crisp. Drain and crumble to measure ⅔ cup. Return the bacon to the soup pot. Add the onions and cook for 5 minutes until soft and transparent. Blend in the flour. Gradually blend in the bouillon. Add the sliced potatoes. Cover and let simmer for 1 hour.

In a medium bowl blend the sour cream with the cream and egg yolks. Spoon a little of the soup into the egg mixture and blend thoroughly. Add the egg mixture to the soup. Heat, stirring constantly, for 5 minutes, making sure it does not come to a boil. Add the parsley. Serve warm.

Makes 6 servings.

Elvis signing his movie contract.

Elvis and Debra Paget enjoying lunch on the set.

Minestrone Soup

3 quarts boiling water	¼ cup packed light brown sugar
3 potatoes, sliced	3 tablespoons butter
3 small onions, chopped	3 tablespoons olive oil
¼ head cabbage, shredded	2 tablespoons Parmesan cheese,
½ pound string beans	grated
2 cups macaroni shells	1 clove garlic, minced
2 cups kidney beans, drained	Salt and pepper to taste
1 cup chopped celery	¼ cup cream

In a soup pot with the boiling water cook the potatoes, onions, cabbage, and string beans. Add the macaroni and continue cooking for 20 minutes. Add the kidney beans, chopped celery, and brown sugar. Continue to cook until the celery is tender.

In a medium bowl cream together the butter and olive oil. Blend in the Parmesan cheese, garlic, salt, pepper, and cream. Add the creamed mixture to the vegetable and macaroni mixture. Continue cooking until well blended.

Makes 6 servings.

Cream of Celery Soup

1½ cups water
2 cups diced celery
1 onion, chopped
¼ teaspoon salt

¼ cup butter
¼ cup all-purpose flour
4 cups milk
1 teaspoon salt

In a saucepan boil the water. Add the celery and onion and simmer for 10 minutes. Add the ¼ teaspoon salt. In a separate saucepan melt the butter. Blend in the flour. Gradually add the milk. Cook, stirring constantly, until the sauce boils and becomes thick and smooth. Drain the water from the celery and onion and add it to the sauce with the remaining salt. Heat to boiling.

Makes 4 servings.

*E*lvis liked to snack on such things as meatball sandwiches, peanut-butter-and-mashed banana sandwiches, and ice cream with Pepsi Cola. Due to his busy schedule, he couldn't sit down to a formal dinner very often. But in those rare instances when he did, he liked simple, home-style food such as roast or steak with potatoes and gravy, bread, and butter. Potatoes and a small steak was a fancy meal to Elvis. ■

Elvis with Debra Paget at the 20th Century Fox studio commissary.

Potato with Cheese Soup

1 potato
3 cups hot water
2 beef bouillon cubes
2 cups milk
1 cup cream
3 tablespoons all-purpose flour

2 to 4 tablespoons butter
½ pound grated Cheddar cheese
1½ teaspoons minced onion
1¼ teaspoons salt
Worcestershire sauce

Scrub, peel, and dice the potato. In a 3-quart saucepan cover the potato with the hot water. Cook until the potato is tender and falls easily from a fork. Drain the water, reserving 2 cups. Push the potato through a sieve. Return the potato and reserved potato water to the pan. Add the bouillon cubes, milk, and cream, and heat through. Add the flour and butter. Blend thoroughly, stirring constantly, until thick. Let the soup boil for 2 minutes. Add the cheese, onion, and salt. Add the Worcestershire sauce to taste. Serve warm.

Makes 4 cups.

Chicken Soup

⅔ cup asparagus tips
2 tablespoons butter, softened
2 tablespoons all-purpose flour
4 cups strained chicken stock
2 cups cooked chicken, diced

½ cup fresh green peas
½ cup diced celery
Salt and pepper to taste
½ cup evaporated milk

Clean and dice the asparagus. In a medium bowl blend the softened butter with the flour. In a saucepan heat the chicken stock just to the boiling point. Add the asparagus, chicken, peas, and celery. Simmer for 10 minutes or until the vegetables become tender. Blend in the butter and flour. Continue stirring until thick and smooth. Season with the salt and pepper. Blend in the evaporated milk.

Makes 4 servings.

Chicken Gumbo

1½ cups okra
3 tablespoons butter
¼ cup diced green bell pepper
¼ cup minced onion
4 cups chicken stock

2½ cups stewed tomatoes
Salt and pepper to taste
2 tablespoons chopped parley
1 cup diced cooked chicken

Cut the okra into ½-inch pieces. In a soup pot heat the butter and sauté the green bell pepper, okra, and onion for 10 minutes. Add the chicken stock and stewed tomatoes. Boil for 10 minutes or until the vegetables are tender. Season with the salt and pepper. Add the parsley and chicken, and continue to cook until the chicken is thoroughly heated.

Makes 6 servings.

Fans visiting Elvis on the set of Love Me Tender.

Elvis visiting with fans while he enjoys a snack.

*O*ne Saturday Elvis went to catch Sammy Davis Jr.'s show at the Moulin Rouge. Arriving at the nightclub, Elvis met Hal Wallis and joined him for dinner. Elvis was impressed that in his final act Sammy included an impersonation of him. Because so many fans were in the lobby of the hotel, Elvis had to leave through the kitchen by way of a freight elevator.

Later, Elvis invited Sammy back to his hotel suite at the Beverly Wilshire. Elvis ordered pizza from a restaurant around the corner, and they talked and ate until 2:00 A.M. ■

*E*lvis Presley ate just about the same lunch every day at the studio commissary: lots of mashed potatoes with gravy, sauerkraut, crisp bacon, and two glasses of milk. For dessert he liked fruit gelatin with whipped cream. ■

Hamburger Soup

1½ pounds ground beef
6 cups water
3 cups diced potatoes
1 cup diced celery
½ cup diced onion

2 cups stewed tomatoes
¼ cup rice
2 beef bouillon cubes
¾ teaspoon salt
Pepper to taste

In a skillet brown the ground beef. Drain off all fat. In a soup pot bring the water to a boil. Add the potatoes, celery, onion, tomatoes, rice, bouillon cubes, and the cooked ground beef. Cover and bring to a boil a second time. Reduce the heat to medium and let the soup cook for 30 minutes. Add the salt and pepper.

Makes 6 servings.

*S*hortly after her first invitation to the Presley Bel Air mansion, a young starlet commented in surprise, "I thought when he invited me to dinner that there would be just the two of us sitting across a candlelit table. But I couldn't have been more wrong. I found out that an 'intimate' dinner in Elvis's book consists of him, the girls he's asked to dine with him, and all six of his boys."

The meal itself was far from what she had expected. "You sit around a huge dining room table where you are served huge helpings of roast beef, black-eyed peas, corn muffins, sliced tomatoes, and orange soda pop." ■

Elvis getting help with his hat from Debra Paget.

Fruit Salad

1 medium-sized pineapple
2 medium apples
3 bananas

1 cup strawberries
½ pound grapes
Fresh lemon juice

Peel and core the pineapple. Cut into 1-inch bite-size pieces. Peel and core the apples. Cut into quarters and dice into bite-size pieces. Peel and slice the bananas. Remove the stems from the strawberries and slice. Slice the grapes. In a large bowl toss the fruit in as much natural juice as possible. Add a dash of fresh lemon juice. Serve on beds of shredded lettuce.

Makes 4 servings.

Elvis waiting for his next scene.

*I*t seemed to anyone who knew Elvis that he went out of his way to be friendly. He didn't put on airs just because he was Elvis Presley. So on the first day of shooting, he let it slip to the director that he had memorized everyone's lines, not just his own. He wanted to show that he was willing to work hard to become a good actor. ■

Elvis and Robert Wagner in the studio commissary.

Chef's Salad

½ head iceberg lettuce
½ head Bibb lettuce
6 slices bacon
2 tomatoes
1 slice thick ham

2 cups cooked chicken, diced
1 avocado, diced
3 hard-boiled eggs
½ cup grated Cheddar cheese
1 tablespoon chives

Wash the lettuce under cold running water. Pat dry with paper towels. In a large bowl tear the lettuce into bite-size pieces. In a skillet fry the bacon until crisp. Drain the fat and crumble. Let cool.

Chop the tomatoes and add them to the lettuce. Slice the ham into strips. Add the ham, chicken, avocado, eggs, cheese, and bacon to the lettuce. Season with the chives. Serve with favorite salad dressing.

Makes 4 servings.

Tossed Green Salad

½ head iceberg lettuce	Salt and pepper to taste
1 large tomato, chopped	2 hard-boiled eggs
¼ cup shredded cabbage	½ cup shredded carrots
½ cup chopped celery	

Wash the lettuce under cold running water. Pat dry with paper towels. In a medium bowl tear the lettuce into bite-size pieces. Add the tomato, cabbage, and celery. Refrigerate about 20 minutes.

Before serving toss with favorite salad dressing. Season with the salt and pepper. Dice the eggs and crumble them over the top of the salad. Garnish with the shredded carrots.

Makes 2 servings.

On a date with Cathy Case, a girl he met in Hollywood, Elvis went to the Moulin Rouge to see Jerry Lewis. ■

Cole Slaw

2 tablespoons sugar	¾ cup milk
½ teaspoon salt	¼ cup vinegar
1 teaspoon dry mustard	1 tablespoon butter
1½ tablespoons all-purpose flour	1 head cabbage, grated
1 egg, beaten	

In the top of a double boiler over simmering water combine the sugar, salt, dry mustard, and flour. Add the egg and milk, mixing well. Add the vinegar a little at a time. Continue stirring until thick. Add the butter and blend thoroughly. Let the dressing cool. Refrigerate.

With a sharp knife chop the cabbage into fine shreds. Add 1 cup of dressing to 4 cups of shredded cabbage. Season with the salt and pepper. Toss to coat the cabbage thoroughly. Refrigerate about 1 hour before serving.

Makes 4 servings.

Fruit Gelatin with Cream

1 6-ounce box strawberry-banana flavored gelatin
1 15½-ounce can fruit cocktail

Heavy cream, whipped
Shredded lettuce

Make the gelatin according to the package directions. Drain the syrup from the fruit cocktail. Add the fruit to the gelatin. Pour into a mold and refrigerate until firm.

Beat the cream until smooth and somewhat thick. Unmold the gelatin and place it on a bed of shredded lettuce. Spoon the whipped cream in the center of the mold.

Makes 6 servings.

Potato Salad

4 medium potatoes, peeled and sliced
1 medium white onion, diced
⅓ cup diced celery
¼ cup diced red bell pepper

½ tablespoon sugar
2 tablespoons vinegar
¾ cup mayonnaise
Salt

In a stock pot boil the potatoes in hot salted water. Let them cool throughly.

In a medium bowl toss together the onion, celery, and red bell pepper with the potatoes. Add the sugar and vinegar. Coat with the mayonnaise. More mayonnaise may be added to achieve the desired consistency. Season with the salt. Refrigerate about 1 hour.

Makes 4 servings.

Macaroni Salad

1 pound salad macaroni, (shells, spirals, or elbow)
1 cup diced celery
1½ cups mayonnaise

2 tablespoons mustard
1 4-ounce can diced black olives
Salt and pepper to taste
3 tablespoons dill pickle juice

Prepare the macaroni according to package directions. Let it cool thoroughly.

In a medium bowl blend the celery, mayonnaise, mustard, and olives. Season with the salt and pepper. Add the dill pickle juice. Toss with the cold macaroni. Refrigerate for about 1 hour before serving.

Makes 6 servings.

Hot Chicken Salad

2 cups cubed cooked chicken
1 cup mayonnaise
¼ cup mushrooms, sliced
2 tablespoons minced onion
1½ cup diced celery

2 tablespoons fresh lemon juice
½ teaspoon salt
½ cup chopped walnuts
½ cup grated Cheddar cheese

In a medium bowl toss the chicken with the mayonnaise. Add the mushrooms, onion, and celery. Blend in the lemon juice, salt, and walnuts. Place the salad in a casserole dish. Sprinkle the grated cheese over the top. Bake at 450° for 20 minutes or until the cheese has melted.

Makes 4 servings.

While working on a film, Elvis customarily ate lunch in his dressing room or at the studio commissary. ∎

Almond Chicken Salad

3 cups cubed cooked chicken
½ cup sliced almonds
⅓ cup seedless grapes

½ cup mayonnaise
1¼ teaspoons vinegar
Salt and pepper

In a medium bowl combine the cooked chicken with the almonds and grapes. Toss lightly. Add the mayonnaise and vinegar. Season with the salt and pepper. Blend all the ingredients together thoroughly. Refrigerate about 1 hour before serving. Serve on beds of shredded lettuce.

Makes 4 servings.

An early publicity photo

Ham & Chicken Salad

2 cups cubed cooked chicken
1½ cups cubed cooked ham
1 cup diced celery
1 tablespoon chopped sweet
   pickle

1½ cups mayonnaise
2 teaspoons mustard
1 tablespoon fresh lemon juice
Salt and pepper to taste

In a medium bowl combine the chicken and ham. Toss thoroughly.
Add the celery and sweet pickle. In a separate bowl blend together
the mayonnaise, mustard, and lemon juice. Add the chicken and
ham mixture and toss. Season with the salt and pepper.
   Makes 6 servings.

Bacon & Egg Salad

3 slices bacon	1 cup diced celery
8 eggs, hard boiled	1 cup diced cucumber
7 tablespoons mayonnaise	Salt and pepper

In a skillet fry the bacon until crisp. Drain on paper towels. Crumble and set aside to let cool thoroughly.

Peel and finely chop the eggs. In a medium bowl blend the eggs with the mayonnaise, celery, and cucumber. Mix in the crumbled bacon. Season with the salt and pepper.

Makes 4 servings.

*W*hile filming *Love Me Tender* in 1956, Elvis and his entourage of friends took up an entire floor of the Knickerbocker Hotel on Ivar Avenue. They stayed there through mid-October. ■

Cobb Salad

1 pound bacon	6 tablespoons white wine
1 avocado	vinegar
Fresh lemon juice	½ cup oil
2 eggs, hard boiled	Salt and pepper to taste
1 tomato	½ cup blue cheese
1 head iceberg lettuce	

In a skillet fry the bacon until crisp. Drain on paper towels. Crumble and set aside. Peel and dice the avocado. Sprinkle with lemon juice and set it aside. Peel and dice the eggs and set them aside. Core and dice the tomato and set it aside.

Shred the lettuce into fine strips. In a small bowl combine the vinegar with the oil. Season with the salt and pepper. Pour the dressing over the shredded lettuce and toss thoroughly.

Arrange the lettuce in the bottom of a large bowl. Crumble the blue cheese and place it in the center of the lettuce. Surround the cheese with sections of the bacon, avocado, egg, tomato, and chicken.

Makes 4 servings.

Elvis receives an award for "Don't Be Cruel" from Billboard *magazine.*

*I*n 1957 Elvis answered these questions from his fans:

What is your favorite food?
"I like pork chops or ham and sauerkraut and a mess of mashed potatoes. Since I really don't have a lot of time to eat, I like a lot of sandwiches."
What do you do for fun in Hollywood?
"I like to watch movies. Maybe I'll go shoot some pool. And I love to ride my motorcycle." ■

Cucumber Salad

½ cup sugar
¾ cup sour cream
2 tablespoons vinegar

Salt and pepper to taste
2 cups thinly sliced cucumbers

In a medium bowl blend the sugar with the sour cream and vinegar. Season with the salt and pepper. Toss in the sliced cucumbers, making sure to coat well. Refrigerate before serving.
Makes 4 servings.

oving You, for Paramount, was Elvis's second film and producer Hal Wallis's first with Elvis. The script was written with Elvis in mind. ■

Picnic Salad

4 slices bacon
1 head romaine lettuce
3 cups diced potatoes
2 tomatoes
3 hard-boiled eggs

¾ cups diced celery
2 tablespoons minced onion
Mayonnaise
¼ teaspoon salt
6 green bell pepper rings

In a skillet fry the bacon until crisp. Drain on paper towels. Crumble and set aside. Wash the lettuce and dry it with paper towels. Boil the potatoes until soft. Dice the tomatoes. Slice the eggs.
Line a platter with the lettuce leaves. In a medium bowl combine the potatoes, celery, onion, and bacon. Toss gently. Mix in the mayonnaise for taste and consistency. Add the salt. Place on top of the lettuce leaves. Garnish with the tomatoes, eggs, and green bell pepper rings. Refrigerate before serving.
Makes 4 servings.

Elvis trying out his cowboy boots for the
"Teddy Bear" segment of Loving You.

*F*or a night out, Elvis decided to head over to the Coconut Grove in Hollywood. When he arrived, he met Milton Berle. "One of the first television shows I appeared on was his. He was a good friend to me." ■

Green Bean Salad

½ pound green beans, cut into
   ½-inch slices
1 cup boiling water
½ teaspoon salt
1 hard-boiled egg

2 tablespoons sweet pickle
¼ cup diced celery
2 tablespoons minced radishes
1 tablespoon fresh lemon juice
¼ cup mayonnaise

In a soup pot cook the beans in the water, adding the salt. Cook for 7 minutes, until tender. Remove the pan from the stove and let the beans cool in the pot.

Drain the liquid. Dice the egg. In a medium bowl toss the eggs with the sweet pickle, celery, and radishes. Add the beans, lemon juice, and mayonnaise. Toss gently to coat the beans. Refrigerate before serving.

Makes 4 servings.

Baked Bean & Sauerkraut Salad

2 ½ cups sauerkraut
2 tablespoons bacon drippings
2 cups baked beans

⅔ cup water
1 teaspoon sugar
¼ teaspoon caraway

In a saucepan combine the sauerkraut, bacon drippings, baked beans, and water. Simmer over very low heat for 10 minutes. Stir frequently to blend the sauerkraut with the beans. Add the sugar and caraway seeds. Serve warm.

Makes 4 servings.

Baked Bean Salad

3 slices bacon
2 cups baked beans
2 sweet pickles, chopped

½ cup diced celery
Mayonnaise
2 hard-boiled eggs

In a skillet fry the bacon until crisp. Drain on paper towels. Crumble. In a saucepan heat the baked beans. Add the chopped sweet pickle and celery. Blend in the crumbled bacon. Add desired amount of mayonnaise for a smooth consistency. Garnish with the sliced hard-boiled eggs.

Makes 2 servings.

*M*ary Ann Mobley co-starred with Elvis in two films, *Girl Happy* in 1956 and *Harum Scarum* in 1965.

When was the first time you met Elvis?
"The first time I met Elvis was when we started to work on the movie. It ended up being the beginning of a wonderful friendship. If anyone said anything in front of me that he didn't think was proper, he'd say, 'Don't you ever swear in front of this lady.' He protected me. When I would come onto the set, he'd say, `Where's Mary Ann's chair?' And he would stand up and make sure that I was being taken care of."

What were your first impressions?
"I was very impressed—the first moment—by his kindness. I was very aware that he had a special magic that you couldn't put your finger on. I think it was a great mystery to him as well.

Do you think he knew he had some kind of magic?
"I think he must have known he had it, but not in a pompous way. He never appeared pompous or conceited. He must have wondered what it was himself. He had to have thought that he had some kind of magic because people came to see him and supported him the way they did."

What types of things would you talk about?
"When we sat and talked, we would talk about Mississippi since we were both from there. We used to talk about southern cooking, things like fried okra and other food people out here had never heard about. Sometimes we'd talk about acting. I got the feeling that he really felt he could do better acting than he was given the chance to do.

What was he like on the set?
"I never saw or heard him throw his weight around on the set. He was always a perfect gentleman. He always knew his lines, and he was always on time."

Do you have a particular memory of Elvis?
"At the end of one day, I was walking to my car and Elvis and the guys were walking to his, and he said, 'Mary Ann, one of these days I'm going to have a party that I can invite you to.' He put women up on a pedestal, and I was very fortunate because I feel he put me up on a pedestal. He treated me with great respect. I remember him with great fondness." ∎

BREADS

White Bread

1 envelope active dry yeast
¾ cup warm water (110°)
1 teaspoon sugar
2 cups milk
2 tablespoons sugar

1½ teaspoons salt
2 tablespoons shortening
6 cups all-purpose flour, sifted
Butter, melted

Grease two loaf pans and set them aside.

In a small bowl stir together the yeast and water. Add 1 teaspoon of sugar. Set aside for about 5 minutes.

In a saucepan heat the milk just to boiling. In a mixing bowl combine the milk, remaining sugar, salt, and shortening. Cool to lukewarm. Add the yeast mixture and 3 cups of sifted flour. Beat well. Add more flour to make a soft dough.

Place the remaining flour on a board. Turn the dough onto the floured surface and knead until smooth and elastic. Place in a greased bowl, turning so the greased side is on top. Cover with a cloth and set the dough aside until it has doubled in bulk. Punch down and let the dough rise again.

Cut the dough into halves. Shape into smooth rounded balls. Cover with a cloth and let stand for 10 minutes. Shape into loaves and place in the prepared pans. Brush the tops with melted butter.

Cover with a cloth and set aside until double in bulk. Bake at 400° for 10 minutes. Reduce the heat to 375° and bake for 40 minutes.

Makes 2 loaves.

Dinner Rolls

1½ cups warm water (110°)
1 envelope active dry yeast
¾ cup milk, scalded
¼ cup sugar

2 teaspoons salt
2 tablespoons butter
6 cups all-purpose flour, sifted

In a large mixing bowl stir together the water and yeast. Set the mixture aside for about 5 minutes.

Blend in the milk, sugar, and salt. Add the butter and 3 cups of flour, and blend until well mixed. Add the remaining flour. Mix the dough until it becomes stiff and takes on the shape of a ball.

Roll out the dough to ¼-inch thickness. Cut into circles 2 inches in diameter with a biscuit cutter. Place about 1 inch apart on a baking sheet. Make a small crease across the center. Cover with a cloth and let the rolls rise until double in bulk.

Brush with the melted butter. Fold the smaller side over the larger. Press ends together to form a crease. Bake at 400° for 15 minutes or until brown.

Makes 2 dozen.

Elvis on the set of The Trouble with Girls.

Signing autographs at a gas station in Van Nuys, California.

Bread Sticks

1 envelope active dry yeast
¾ cup warm water (110°)
1½ tablespoons sugar
1 cup milk

¼ teaspoon salt
¼ cup butter
1 egg white
3½ cups all-purpose flour, sifted

In a small bowl stir together the yeast and water. Add 1 teaspoon of sugar. Set aside for about 5 minutes. In a mixing bowl blend the milk, sugar, salt, and butter. Add the yeast mixture, egg white, and half the sifted flour. Add more flour to make a soft dough.

Place the remaining flour on a board. Turn the dough onto the floured surface and knead until smooth and elastic. Place in a greased bowl, turning so the greased side is on top. Cover with a cloth and let the dough rise until it has doubled in bulk. Punch down and let the dough rise again. Shape into thin sticks and place them on a greased baking sheet. Let the dough rise once more. Bake at 400° for about 10 minutes. Reduce the heat to 325° and continue baking until the sticks become dry and crisp.

Makes 18 sticks.

Cheese Bread

1 package active dry yeast	2 tablespoons sugar
¼ cup warm water (110°)	2½ cups grated Cheddar cheese
1½ cups skim milk	1 teaspoon salt
¼ cup grated carrot	5 cups all-purpose flour
3 tablespoons oil	

In a small bowl stir together the yeast and water. Set aside for 5 minutes, then stir to dissolve the yeast.

In a saucepan combine the milk, carrot, oil, sugar, cheese, and salt. Cook until the mixture becomes warm. Pour over the yeast. Add 3½ cups of flour. Add more of the flour as needed to create a stiff dough.

Turn onto a floured board. Add flour as necessary if dough is sticky. Knead until smooth. Place in a greased bowl. Turn once so the greased side is on top. Cover and let double in bulk. Punch down and shape into 2 loaves.

Put in two 9 x 5-inch loaf pans. Let the loaves rise again until doubled in bulk. Bake at 350° for 40 minutes.

Makes 2 loaves.

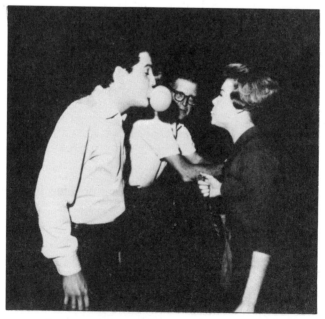

Showing Hope Lange how to blow a bubble.

Banana Nut Bread

¼ cup vegetable oil
1 cup sugar
2 eggs, beaten
3 bananas, mashed
2 cups all-purpose flour
1 teaspoon baking soda

½ teaspoon baking powder
¼ teaspoon salt
3 tablespoons milk
½ teaspoon vanilla extract
½ cup chopped walnuts

Line a loaf pan with waxed paper and set it aside.

In a mixing bowl beat together the vegetable oil and sugar. Add the eggs and bananas and beat well. In a separate bowl sift together the flour, baking soda, baking powder, and salt. Mix the dry ingredients into the banana mixture. Add the milk and vanilla. Beat thoroughly. Add the walnuts.

Pour batter into the prepared pan. Bake at 350° for 1 hour. Let cool.

Makes 1 loaf.

Molasses Bread

2 cups all-purpose flour
1 teaspoon salt
1 teaspoon baking soda
¾ teaspoon baking powder
½ cup dark molasses
⅓ cup sugar

3 tablespoons butter, melted
1½ teaspoons lemon rind
1 tablespoon fresh lemon juice
½ cup chopped walnuts
⅔ cup buttermilk

Grease a 9 x 5-inch baking pan and set it aside.

In a mixing bowl sift the flour. Measure 2 cups and resift 3 more times with the salt, baking soda, and baking powder. In a separate mixing bowl combine the molasses, sugar, melted butter, lemon rind, and lemon juice. Beat until well blended. Add the chopped nuts. Blend in the dry ingredients alternately with the buttermilk to the egg mixture. Mix thoroughly after each addition.

Pour the batter into prepared pan. Let the batter stand 15 minutes. Cover with a pan of the same size. Preheat the oven for 10 minutes at 350°. Bake for 20 minutes. Remove the cover and bake an additional 40 minutes or until a toothpick inserted in the center comes out clean. Remove to rack and let cool.

Makes 1 loaf.

Oatmeal Raisin Bread

2 cups all-purpose flour
2½ teaspoons baking powder
¾ teaspoon baking soda
1 teaspoon salt
1 cup raisins

1 cup oats
2 tablespoons molasses
1¼ cups buttermilk
¼ cup packed light brown sugar
2 tablespoons butter, melted

Grease a loaf pan and set it aside.

In a mixing bowl sift the flour. Add the baking powder, baking soda, and salt. Sift again. Add the raisins and oats, and mix thoroughly. In a separate bowl mix together the molasses, buttermilk, brown sugar, and butter. Add the liquid mixture to the flour mixture. Stir just to moisten the flour.

Pour the batter into the prepared pan. Bake at 350° for 1 hour. Let cool before serving.

Makes 1 loaf.

Peach Bread

1 envelope active dry yeast
¼ cup warm water (110°)
2 cups milk, scalded
2 tablespoons butter
1 tablespoon sugar

3 teaspoons salt
6 cups all-purpose flour, sifted
1½ cups peaches
1 tablespoon fresh lemon juice

Grease 2 loaf pans and set them aside. In a small bowl stir together the yeast and water. Let stand about 5 minutes. In a separate bowl combine the milk, butter, sugar, and salt. Let cool until slightly warm.

In a large mixing bowl combine the yeast with the cooled milk mixture. Add 3 cups of flour. Beat until smooth and the batter becomes thin. Add the peaches mixed with the lemon juice. Add additional flour to make a stiff dough. Mix thoroughly.

Turn the dough onto a floured board. Knead for 10 minutes or until the dough is smooth. Place the dough in a warmed, greased bowl. Brush the surface with melted butter. Cover and let rise until it has doubled in bulk.

Punch the dough down. Turn out on a floured board. Divide in half. Mold into smooth round balls. Cover for 10 minutes. Shape into loaves.

Place in the prepared pans. Brush with melted butter. Cover and let rise until doubled in bulk. Bake at 375° for 45 minutes.

Makes 2 loaves.

Elvis with Colonel Tom Parker at a cast party for
Wild in the Country, *also Elvis's twenty-sixth birthday.*

Apple Coffee Cake

1½ cups all-purpose flour
2¼ teaspoons baking powder
½ cup sugar
½ teaspoon salt
½ teaspoon ground cinnamon
1 egg
½ cup milk

¼ cup butter, melted
1½ cups chopped, peeled, tart
  apples
¼ cup sugar
2 tablespoons all-purpose flour
½ teaspoon ground cinnamon
1 tablespoon butter

Grease an 8-inch cake pan and set it aside.

In a mixing bowl sift 1½ cups of flour. Measure and resift 3 more times with the baking powder, ½ cup of sugar, salt, and ½ teaspoon of cinnamon. In a separate bowl beat the egg. Add the milk and ¼ cup of melted butter. Pour the liquid mixture into the dry ingredients. Add the apples. Blend thoroughly.

Pour the batter into the prepared pan. In a mixing bowl blend ¼ cup of sugar, 2 tablespoons of flour, and ½ teaspoon of cinnamon for the topping. Add 1 tablespoon of butter, and mix until crumbly. Sprinkle the topping over the batter. Bake at 400° for 30 minutes or until a toothpick inserted in the center comes out clean.

Makes 6 servings.

Elvis looking at the many products that were sold under his name.

*T*he Colonel engaged Special Projects, Inc., in Beverly Hills to handle all of Elvis's product merchandising. Before it was over, no less than seventy-eight different Elvis products were being sold, and millions of dollars in sales were reported each month.

The marketing was so pervasive that if one of Elvis's fans bought one of everything, upon rising in the morning she could put on Elvis Presley bobby socks, Elvis Presley shoes, an Elvis Presley skirt, an Elvis Presley blouse, and an Elvis Presley sweater. She could hang an Elvis Presley charm bracelet from one wrist, put an Elvis Presley handkerchief in her Elvis Presley purse, and head for school. Here she might swap some Elvis Presley bubble gum before class, where she would take notes with an Elvis Presley pencil.

After school she might change into Elvis Presley Bermuda shorts, Elvis Presley blue jeans (which were not blue but black, trimmed in white, and carried Elvis's face on a pocket tag), or Elvis Presley toreador pants. Then she might either write to an Elvis Presley pen pal (whose address she got from an Elvis Presley magazine) or play an Elvis Presley game while drinking an Elvis Presley soft drink.

Before going to bed in her Elvis Presley knit pajamas, she might write in her Elvis Presley diary, using an Elvis Presley ballpoint pen, while listening to "Hound Dog" a final ten times. When she switched out the light, she could watch a glow-in-the-dark Elvis Presley picture. ■

Blueberry Coffee Cake

2 cups all-purpose flour	½ teaspoon salt
¾ cup sugar	¼ cup butter
1 cup fresh or frozen blueberries	2 eggs, beaten
3½ teaspoons baking powder	¾ cup milk

Grease an 8-inch baking pan and set it aside.

In a mixing bowl sift the flour and remeasure 2 cups. Mix 2 tablespoons of the flour with ¼ cup sugar. Add the mixture to the blueberries. To the remaining flour add the baking powder and salt. Sift again. In a separate bowl blend the butter with the remaining sugar. Continue to blend until the dough is light. Add the eggs. Mix thoroughly. Add the flour mixture alternately with the milk. Stir in the blueberries. Blend but do not beat.

Pour batter into the prepared pan. Bake at 375° for 35 minutes. Let cool. Before serving cut into squares.

Makes 6 servings.

Cherry Coffee Cake

1 envelope active dry yeast	3 eggs, beaten
¼ cup warm water (110°)	1 teaspoon vanilla extract
⅔ cup sugar	Melted butter
1 cup milk, scalded	3 cups pitted sour cherries
3½ cups all-purpose flour, sifted	3 tablespoons sugar
⅓ cup butter	1 teaspoon ground cinnamon
1 teaspoon salt	

Grease 2 11 x 7-inch baking pans well and set them aside.

In a mixing bowl add the yeast to the warm water. Add 1 teaspoon of sugar. Set aside for about 10 minutes.

In a mixing bowl sift the flour. Blend together the yeast, milk, and 1½ cups of flour until smooth. Cover and let rise in a warm place about 45 minutes.

In a separate bowl cream together the butter, salt, and remaining sugar. Beat until smooth. Add the yeast mixture. Blend in the eggs and vanilla. Add the remaining flour. Mix thoroughly.

Spread the batter in the prepared pans. Brush the batter with melted butter. Lay the cherries close together pressing slightly into the batter. Mix together the sugar and cinnamon. Sprinkle the mixture over the top. Cover and let rise until double in bulk, about 1 hour.

Cover the pan. Bake at 400° for 10 minutes. Remove the cover and continue to bake about 20 minutes more. Serve warm.

Makes 8 servings.

Cinnamon Coffee Cake

2 cups sifted cake flour
2½ teaspoons baking powder
½ teaspoon salt
⅓ cup butter
1 cup sugar
1 teaspoon vanilla extract

1 egg
⅔ cup milk
1 cup sugar
2 tablespoons ground
  cinnamon

Grease 2 8-inch cake pans and set them aside.

In a mixing bowl sift together the cake flour, baking powder, and salt. In a separate mixing bowl cream the butter with 1 cup of sugar until fluffy. Add the vanilla and well-beaten egg. Add the flour mixture alternately with the milk. Beat until smooth.

Mix the cinnamon with the remaining sugar. Sprinkle the cinnamon mixture in the bottom of the prepared pans. Pour the batter equally between the 2 pans. Bake at 350° for 30 minutes. Let the cake cool before serving.

Makes 8 servings.

Pecan Rolls

3 cups all-purpose flour
4½ teaspoons baking powder
¾ teaspoon salt
⅓ cup sugar
½ cup butter
⅔ cup milk
2 eggs

¼ cup sugar
1 teaspoon ground cinnamon
¼ cup butter
¾ cup packed light brown sugar
2 tablespoons corn syrup
⅓ cup pecan halves

In a large bowl sift the flour with the baking powder, salt, and ⅓ cup of sugar. Blend in one-half of the butter. Add the milk and eggs. Mix until the flour mixture is moist. Turn the dough onto a floured board and knead 10 times. Roll into a rectangle about ¼-inch thick. Brush with 2 tablespoons of melted butter.

In a separate bowl blend ¼ cup of sugar with the cinnamon. Sprinkle over the top. Roll the dough up and seal the edges. Cut into slices ¾-inch thick. In a saucepan melt ¼ cup of butter. Add the brown sugar and corn syrup. Spoon some of the syrup into the bottom of 18 muffin cups. Add the pecan halves. Place a slice of dough into each muffin cup. Bake at 375° for 25 minutes. Remove from pan while still warm.

Makes 18.

Cinnamon Pinwheels

2 cups all-purpose flour, sifted
2 teaspoons baking powder
1 teaspoon salt
⅓ cup shortening
¾ cup buttermilk

2 tablespoons butter, melted
¾ cup packed light brown sugar
1 teaspoon ground cinnamon
¼ cup chopped walnuts

Grease a baking sheet and set it aside.

In a mixing bowl sift together the flour, baking powder, and salt. Cut in the shortening, mixing until it resembles cornmeal. Make a well in the center of the dough and pour in the buttermilk. Stir with a fork. Place the dough onto a floured board and knead for 15 minutes.

Roll out the dough into a rectangle shape about ¼-inch thick. Brush with the melted butter. In a small bowl mix the brown sugar with the cinnamon and walnuts. Sprinkle the mixture over the dough. Roll the dough and press down the edges to seal. Cut into 1-inch slices. Place the slices flat on the prepared baking sheet. Bake at 450° for 10 minutes.

Makes 2 dozen.

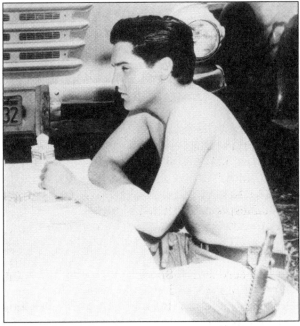

Taking a quick break on the set of Flaming Star.

Peanut Butter Pinwheels

2 cups all-purpose flour
3 teaspoons baking powder
1 teaspoon salt
¼ cup butter

½ cup milk
2 tablespoons butter, melted
½ cup creamy peanut butter

Grease a baking sheet and set it aside.

In a mixing bowl sift the flour. Remeasure and resift, adding the baking powder and salt. Add the butter. Mix until the dough resembles cornmeal. Add the milk to make a soft dough. Add more if needed. The dough should leave the side of the bowl and all of the flour should be blended.

Turn the dough out onto a floured board. Knead the dough for 30 seconds. Turn so the smooth side is facing upward. Roll to ½-inch thickness. Mix together the melted butter and peanut butter. Spread the mixture over the dough. Roll and slice. Place the pinwheels on the prepared baking sheet. Bake at 450° for 12 minutes or until golden. Makes 12.

Banana Doughnuts

5 cups all-purpose flour
3 teaspoons baking powder
1 teaspoon baking soda
¼ teaspoon salt
½ teaspoon grated nutmeg
¼ cup butter
1 cup sugar

1½ teaspoons vanilla extract
3 eggs, beaten
2 bananas, mashed
½ cup buttermilk
½ cup all-purpose flour
Oil

In a mixing bowl sift the 5 cups of flour. Measure 5 cups and add the baking powder, baking soda, salt, and nutmeg. Resift 3 times. In a separate bowl cream the butter with the sugar. Add the vanilla and eggs. Beat until mixture is light and fluffy. Add the bananas and buttermilk. Mix thoroughly. Add the sifted flour mixture in 3 equal portions. Mix well after each addition.

Refrigerate the dough for 2 hours, until thoroughly chilled. Remove a quarter of the dough at a time from the refrigerator, leaving the rest to chill.

Place the dough onto a floured board using the ½ cup flour as needed. Knead lightly and roll out to ⅜-inch in thickness. Cut with a floured 2½-inch doughnut cutter. Heat the oil 375°. Fry the doughnuts until golden. Drain on paper towels. Repeat until all the dough is used. Makes 3 to 4 dozen.

Brown Sugar Doughnuts

5 cups all-purpose flour, sifted
2 teaspoons baking powder
2 teaspoons baking soda
2 teaspoons ground cinnamon
4 eggs

2 cups packed light brown
   sugar
½ cup sour cream
Oil

In a mixing bowl sift together the flour, baking powder, baking soda, and cinnamon and set the bowl aside.

In a separate bowl beat the eggs until thick. Add the brown sugar and blend well. Add the sour cream. Add the dry ingredients, and mix until well blended. If the dough is a bit sticky add more flour as needed. Refrigerate for 1 hour.

Turn the dough onto a floured board. Roll out to ½-inch thickness. Cut with a floured doughnut cutter. Heat the oil to 375°. Fry the doughnuts for 3 minutes, turning several times during the cooking process. Drain on paper towels.

Makes 2 dozen.

Enjoying a snack.

Buttermilk Doughnuts

3½ cups all-purpose flour
4 teaspoons baking powder
¼ teaspoon salt
¼ teaspoon grated nutmeg
baking soda
2 eggs melted

1 cup sugar
½ teaspoon vanilla extract
1 cup buttermilk
2 tablespoons butter, melted
Oil

In a mixing bowl sift the flour. Measure out 3½ cups and add the baking powder, salt, nutmeg, and baking soda. Resift 3 times. In a separate bowl beat the eggs. Add the sugar and vanilla, continue to beat the mixture for 2 minutes. Blend in the buttermilk and butter, then the flour mixture. Blend until the dough is smooth. Refrigerate for 2 hours, until thoroughly chilled.

Remove a quarter of the dough. Keep the remaining dough refrigerated until needed. Place onto a floured board and roll out to ¼-inch thickness. Cut with a floured 2½-inch doughnut cutter. Heat the oil to 375°. Fry the doughnuts until golden. Drain on paper towels. Repeat until all the dough is used.

Chocolate Doughnuts

1⅓ cups all-purpose flour, sifted
½ teaspoon baking soda
½ teaspoon baking powder
¼ teaspoon salt
Nutmeg
¼ cup semisweet chocolate,
    melted

1 egg
½ cup sugar
⅓ cup sour cream
Oil
Confectioners' sugar

In a mixing bowl sift the flour with the baking soda, baking powder, salt, and nutmeg to taste. Blend in the melted chocolate. In a separate bowl beat the egg and sugar together. Add the sour cream and chocolate mixture.

Heat the oil to 370°. Drop the batter by rounded teaspoons into the hot oil and fry until brown, turning once. Drain on paper towels. When still warm sprinkle with confectioners' sugar.

Makes 2 dozen.

Apple Muffins

2 cups all-purpose flour	1 egg
4 teaspoons baking powder	1 cup milk
¼ teaspoon salt	¾ cup peeled and chopped
½ teaspoon ground cinnamon	apple
⅛ teaspoon grated nutmeg	¼ teaspoon ground cinnamon
⅓ cup butter	2 tablespoons sugar
¼ cup sugar	12 apple wedges

Prepare a greased muffin pan and set it aside.

In a mixing bowl sift the flour. Measure 2 cups and add the baking powder, salt, ½ teaspoon cinnamon, and nutmeg. Resift. In a separate bowl blend the butter with ¼ cup of sugar. Beat until light and fluffy. Add the egg and mix thoroughly. Pour in the milk and ¾ cup of chopped apples. Add to the dry ingredients. Mix to moisten the dry ingredients. Pour the batter into prepared muffin pan, filling each cup ⅔ full. Coat the apple wedges with sugar and place 1 wedge in the center of each muffin cup. Mix together ¼ teaspoon of cinnamon and 2 tablespoons of sugar. Sprinkle over the batter. Bake at 400° for 20 minutes.

Makes 1 dozen.

A photo opportunity for fans on the set of Flaming Star.

Bacon-Corn Muffins

12 slices bacon	2 eggs, separated
1½ cups yellow cornmeal	1⅓ cups buttermilk
1 teaspoon salt	2 tablespoons butter
¾ teaspoon baking soda	

In a skillet fry the bacon just until brown. Do not overcook. Drain and set aside.

In a large bowl measure out the cornmeal and sift it with the salt and baking soda. Sift 3 more times. Beat the egg yolks until well blended. Add the buttermilk and continue beating. Add the liquid mixture to the cornmeal and blend until the batter is smooth. Melt the butter and add while hot to the batter. Fold in the stiffly beaten egg whites.

Cut the bacon strips in half. Crisscross two strips of bacon in the bottom of each cup in the muffin pan. Pour batter on top, filling each cup about ⅔ full. Bake at 450° for 25 minutes or until brown. Let the muffins cool somewhat before removing from the pan. Serve warm.

Makes 1 dozen.

Elvis going over the musical arrangement for Wild in the Country.

Coconut Muffins

2 cups all-purpose flour	2 tablespoons shredded coconut
2 teaspoons baking powder	1 egg, beaten
½ teaspoon salt	1 cup milk
2 tablespoons sugar	2 tablespoons butter, melted

Grease a muffin pan well and set it aside.

In a medium bowl sift the flour with the baking powder, salt, and sugar. Mix well. Add the shredded coconut. In a separate bowl mix the egg, milk, and butter. Add the liquid mixture to the dry ingredients and mix just to moisten. Pour the batter into the prepared muffin cups, filling each ⅔ full. Bake at 400° for 20 minutes. Let cool. Makes 1 dozen.

Graham Muffins

2 cups graham flour	¾ teaspoon baking soda
2 tablespoons sugar	1 egg
¼ teaspoon salt	1½ cups buttermilk
1¼ teaspoons baking powder	2 tablespoons butter

Grease a muffin pan and set it aside.

In a medium bowl sift together the flour, sugar, salt, baking powder, and baking soda. In a separate bowl beat the egg. Add the buttermilk and butter. Add the egg mixture to the dry ingredients, and mix until the flour is moistened. Pour the batter into the prepared muffin cups, filling each ⅔ full. Bake at 400° for 20 minutes or until a toothpick inserted in the center comes out clean. Makes 1 dozen.

*L*izabeth Scott, who co-starred with Elvis Presley in *Loving You*, said of him, "He's a real nice, down-to-earth guy. That's why a lot of other actors will help him out and advise him when otherwise they might be jealous." ■

With Tuesday Weld on the set of Wild in the Country.

*T*he Cross Bow, a little-known rock 'n' roll club in San Fernando, was packed solid. Upstairs on the balcony sat Elvis Presley and Tuesday Weld. Earlier they had been spotted having a great time in Pacific Ocean Park eating hot dogs and drinking Pepsi Cola.

Sometimes they would go to one of the so-called greasy spoons around Hollywood to share a hamburger and fries. Neither was picky when it came to eating. And Elvis ordered doubles of the strawberry shortcake to help him regain some of the weight he had lost while in the army. ■

Lemon Muffins

½ cup butter
½ cup sugar
1 cup all-purpose flour
1 teaspoon baking powder
¼ teaspoon baking soda

¼ cup fresh lemon juice
2 eggs, separated
Grated lemon rind
Sugar

Grease a muffin pan and set it aside.

In a medium bowl cream together the butter and sugar until light and fluffy. In a separate bowl mix the flour with the baking powder and baking soda. Add the dry ingredients to the butter mixture alternately with the lemon juice. Beat the egg whites until stiff. Fold the egg whites into the batter along with the lemon rind. Mix just to blend the ingredients.

Pour the batter into prepared muffin cups, filling each ⅔ full. Sprinkle extra sugar over the batter. Bake at 375° for 20 minutes or until golden. Let the muffins cool completely in the pan.

Makes 1 dozen.

Peanut Butter Muffins

1¾ cups all-purpose flour
2½ teaspoons baking powder
2 tablespoons sugar
½ teaspoon salt
¼ cup shortening

¼ cup peanut butter
1 egg, well beaten
¾ cup milk
Strawberry preserves

Grease a muffin pan and set it aside.

In a mixing bowl sift the flour with the baking powder, sugar, and salt. Cut in the shortening and peanut butter with a pastry blender. In a separate bowl mix the egg with the milk. Add the liquid mixture to the dry ingredients and mix just to moisten the flour. Pour the batter into prepared muffin cups, filling each ⅔ full. Place a dab of preserves in the center of each muffin. Bake at 400° for 25 minutes.

Makes 8.

Pineapple Muffins

2 cups all-purpose flour
4 teaspoons baking powder
½ teaspoon salt
¼ cup butter

½ cup sugar
1 egg
1 cup crushed pineapple

Grease a muffin pan and set it aside.

In a medium bowl sift the flour. Remeasure 2 cups and sift again with the baking powder and salt. In a separate bowl cream the butter with the sugar until light and fluffy. Add the egg and continue beating. Mix in the crushed pineapple. Pour the pineapple mixture into the flour mixture. Stir just to moisten the flour. Do not overbeat.

Pour the batter into prepared muffin cups, filling each ⅔ full. Bake at 400° for 20 minutes. Let the muffins cool in the pan.

Makes 1 dozen.

Raisin Muffins

2 cups all-purpose flour
2 teaspoons baking powder
3 tablespoons sugar
1 teaspoon salt

3 tablespoons butter
1 egg
1 cup milk
½ cup raisins

Grease and flour a muffin pan and set it aside.

In a large mixing bowl sift together the flour, baking powder, sugar, and salt. Add the butter and blend slightly. Add the egg and milk. Stir just to blend. Add the raisins. Pour the batter into the prepared muffin cups, filling each ⅔ full. Bake at 400° for 20 minutes.

Makes 1 dozen.

Elvis on the set of Wild in the Country.

Sour Cream Muffins

1 egg
1 cup sour cream
¼ cup milk
2 tablespoons butter, melted
2 cups all-purpose flour

½ teaspoon salt
¼ cup sugar
½ teaspoon baking soda
2 teaspoons baking powder

Grease a muffin pan and set it aside.

In a medium bowl beat the egg. Add the sour cream and milk, and continue to beat until fluffy. Add the melted butter. In a separate bowl sift together the flour, salt, sugar, baking soda, and baking powder. Add the dry ingredients to the liquid batter, and mix until the flour is moistened. Pour the batter into the prepared muffin cups, filling each cup ⅔ full. Bake at 400° for 20 minutes.

Makes 1 dozen.

Hope Lange watching as Elvis goes over the music for Wild in the Country.

Sweet Potato Muffins

1¾ cups all-purpose flour
1 teaspoon salt
3 teaspoons baking powder
1 tablespoon packed light
  brown sugar
½ cup chopped walnuts
2 eggs, well beaten

¾ cup milk
1¼ cups mashed cooked sweet
  potatoes
¼ cup butter, melted
¼ sugar
½ teaspoon cinnamon

Grease a muffin pan and set it aside.

In a medium bowl sift together the flour with the salt and baking powder. Add the brown sugar and chopped walnuts, and mix thoroughly. In a separate bowl combine the eggs, milk, sweet potatoes, and butter. Add the liquid mixture to the dry ingredients and mix until the flour is moistened. Pour the batter into prepared muffin cups, filling each ⅔ full. Bake at 425° for 25 minutes.

In a small bowl combine ¼ cup of sugar with ½ teaspoon of cinnamon. Before serving and while still warm, sprinkle cinnamon-sugar mixture over the top of each muffin.

Makes 18.

Country Pancakes

1 cup all-purpose flour, sifted	2 eggs, separated
1 tablespoon sugar	1 cup buttermilk
½ teaspoon baking powder	2 tablespoons butter, melted
½ teaspoon baking soda	Butter
½ teaspoon salt	Syrup

In a mixing bowl sift the flour, sugar, baking powder, baking soda, and salt. In separate bowls beat the egg whites until stiff and frothy and the egg yolks until thick. Add the buttermilk and 2 tablespoons of melted butter to the egg yolks. Blend until smooth. Pour the liquid mixture into the sifted dry ingredients. Blend well. Add the egg whites.

Heat a griddle pan over low heat. Grease lightly. Pour about ¼ cup of batter onto the hot griddle for each pancake. Fry until bubbles form. Flip over and brown the other side. Serve hot with butter and hot syrup.

Makes 12.

Apricot Fritters

1 cup canned apricots	1 egg
1½ cups all-purpose flour	⅔ cup milk
1½ teaspoons baking powder	Confectioners' sugar
¼ teaspoon salt	Oil
2 tablespoons sugar	

Drain the syrup from the canned apricots. Chop the apricots and set them aside. In a mixing bowl sift the flour. Measure 1½ cups and re-sift 2 times with the baking powder, salt, and sugar. In a separate bowl beat the egg and add the milk. Mix thoroughly. Add egg mixture to the dry ingredients. Beat until the mixture is smooth.

Coat a spoonful of the chopped apricots with the confectioners' sugar. Then coat with the batter so that they are well covered. Heat the oil to 375°. Fry the fritters until golden brown. Drain on paper towels. Repeat until the apricots have been used.

Makes 5 servings.

*T*o Elvis, the real fantasy was success. "I don't know what happened. I just fell into it. My daddy and I were laughing about it the other day. He looked at me and said, 'What happened, El? The last thing I remember, I was working in a can factory and you were driving a truck.' It just caught up with us, but I sure hope it doesn't stop." ∎

Banana Fritters

1¾ cups all-purpose flour
¾ teaspoon baking powder
⅛ teaspoon salt
¼ cup sugar
1 egg

⅓ cup milk
5 medium bananas
Oil
Confectioners' sugar

In a mixing bowl sift the flour. Measure out ¾ cup and resift with the baking powder, salt, and sugar. In a separate bowl beat the egg. Add the milk. Pour the liquid mixture into the flour mixture and mix thoroughly. Peel the bananas, cut in half lengthwise, and cut again across. Dip the banana sections into the batter. Heat the oil to 375°. Fry the fritters until golden brown. Drain on paper towels. Serve warm. Sprinkle with confectioners' sugar.

Makes 5 servings.

*K*ing Creole was the second picture Elvis made with Hal Wallis and was the first film to utilize location shots. Elvis completed the music for the soundtrack and some sound stage shots while in Hollywood. But once those were completed, cast and crew headed for the streets of New Orleans. ∎

Corn Pone

3 cups white cornmeal	¼ cup milk
2 teaspoons salt	1½ cups water
1½ teaspoons baking powder	⅓ cup butter

Grease a baking sheet and set it aside.

In a large bowl combine the cornmeal, salt, and baking powder. Moisten with milk. Add the water to make the batter smooth. Let the batter stand for 8 minutes.

Add the melted butter. Shape the batter into small patties about 4-inches long. Place the patties on the prepared baking sheet. Bake at 425° for 20 minutes. Serve warm.

Makes 18.

*A*mong Elvis's idols were James Dean, Marlon Brando, and Tony Curtis. ■

Cornbread Squares

1 cup all-purpose flour	1 cup yellow cornmeal
1 tablespoon baking powder	1 egg, well beaten
¾ teaspoon salt	1 cup milk
¼ cup sugar	5 tablespoons butter, melted

Lightly grease the bottom of an 8 x 8-inch baking pan and set it aside.

In a mixing bowl sift together the flour, baking powder, salt, and sugar. Add the cornmeal. In a separate bowl blend the egg with the milk. Add the melted butter. Make a well in the center of the dry ingredients and add the liquids. Beat until smooth. Pour the batter into the prepared pan. Bake at 425° for 20 minutes or until the bread tests done. Cut into squares.

Makes 16.

Elvis on location with fans at Lake Pontchartrain in New Orleans, filming King Creole.

Corn Bread Sticks

1⅓ cups all-purpose flour, sifted
¾ cup cornmeal
3 teaspoons baking powder
1 teaspoon salt

3 teaspoons sugar
1 egg, well beaten
1 cup milk
¼ cup vegetable oil

Grease a corn stick pan and set it aside.

In a mixing bowl sift together the flour, cornmeal, baking powder, salt, and sugar. In a separate bowl combine the egg, milk, and oil. Add the flour mixture and stir just to moisten. Pour the batter into the hot prepared pan, filling it ⅔ full. Bake at 425° for 25 minutes. Makes 15.

*I*n his autobiography, Hal Wallis recalled that Elvis was unable to sample some of New Orleans's famous cuisine because of the crowds. Instead, Elvis had to settle for room service. ■

Corn Spoon Bread

¾ cup all-purpose flour
3 teaspoons baking powder
1¼ teaspoons salt
3 tablespoons sugar
1¼ cups yellow cornmeal

2 eggs, beaten
1½ cups milk
1½ cups creamed corn
⅓ cup butter, melted

Grease a casserole dish and set it aside.

In a mixing bowl sift the flour. Add the baking powder, salt, and sugar, and sift again. Add the cornmeal and mix thoroughly. In a separate bowl mix together the eggs, milk, corn, and butter. Add the liquid mixture to the flour mixture and stir just to moisten the flour.

Pour the batter into the prepared dish. Bake at 400° for 50 minutes. Serve warm with butter.

Makes 6 servings.

*W*hile Elvis was in New Orleans filming *King Creole*, he took up the entire tenth floor of the Roosevelt Hotel, just off the French Quarter. The elevator operator was given strict instructions not to let anyone off on that floor because of security.

After an especially long day of shooting, Elvis walked into the elevator and asked the operator for the tenth floor. The operator explained that he could not, under any circumstances, go to the tenth floor because Elvis Presley was staying there. Elvis said he understood but also explained that he was Elvis Presley. The operator looked at Elvis and replied, "I'm sorry, but I cannot stop on that floor for anyone." So Elvis got out on the eleventh floor and walked down a flight of stairs to his suite of rooms. ■

Golden Spoon Bread

4 eggs, separated
2 cups milk, scalded
1 cup yellow cornmeal
1½ cups grated Cheddar cheese

¼ cup butter
1 teaspoon sugar
¼ teaspoon salt

Beat the egg yolks until thick. In a large bowl combine the milk and yellow cornmeal. Add the egg yolks and grated cheese and mix thoroughly. Add the butter, sugar, and salt. In a separate bowl beat the egg whites until thick. Fold the egg whites into the batter, mixing just until blended.

Pour the batter into a casserole dish. Bake at 375° for 35 minutes or until the bread tests done.

Makes 6 servings.

Potato Dumplings

4 medium potatoes
½ cup all-purpose flour
¾ teaspoon salt
¼ teaspoon baking powder

1 egg
Nutmeg
2 tablespoons butter, melted

Wash and peel the potatoes. Place the potatoes in a pot with just enough water to cover the top. Cover the pot and boil until the potatoes fall apart easily when pricked with a fork. Drain well. Dice the potatoes into a large mixing bowl. Let them cool slightly.

In a separate mixing bowl sift together the flour, salt, and baking powder. Drop the egg into the potatoes. Beat well and add the sifted dry ingredients and nutmeg to taste. Mix thoroughly. Shape into a roll 1 inch in diameter. Slice into 1-inch strips.

Drop the dumplings into a pot of boiling salted water. Stir to keep the dumplings from sticking. They should rise to the top. Cook for 8 minutes. Drain and pour melted butter over the top. Serve warm.

Makes 4 servings.

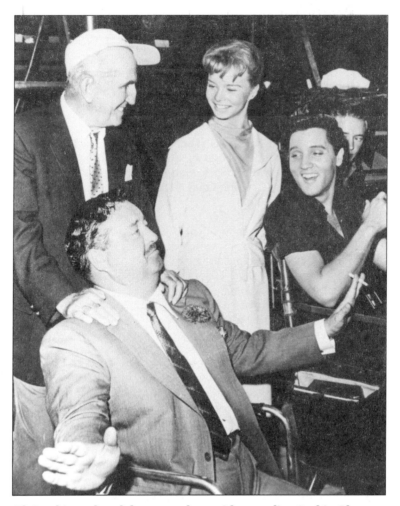

Elvis taking a break between shots with comedian Jackie Gleason.

*E*lvis bought a white Cadillac sedan because he wanted to be able to fit his friends into one car as he drove through the Hollywood hills. He explained, "Last Saturday we all drove down Sunset to catch Bobby Darin's show at The Cloister." ■

*M*arlyn Mason co-starred with Elvis in *The Trouble with Girls* in 1969. Here she shares her memories of Elvis.

When did you first meet Elvis?
"The first time I met Elvis was at one of those rehearsal halls at MGM. He was just wonderful and as nice as could be."

Is it true Elvis liked to play practical jokes on the set?
"I had heard before I met him that he like to set off firecrackers. I told him, 'I've heard about the firecrackers. You'd better watch out.' So he waited. He was always lighting them. You'd be in the middle of a scene, and off in the distance you'd hear, Crack!

"He didn't get me until the very last day, about the last hour. He called me into his trailer. He called me Cap because I wore a cap to work every day, and he said, 'Go on, Cap. Sit down there.' So I sat down, and he started talking to me. All of a sudden a strange feeling came over me, and before I had a chance to jump out of the chair he had tossed a firecracker underneath it. And he said, 'I got you.'"

What is one of your fondest memories about Elvis?
"He was wonderful. He would sing his songs in his trailer. While we were doing the movie, his comeback special aired. I began to listen to his music more and really developed an appreciation for it. Getting the chance to record with him was just a great experience."

What was Elvis like on the set?
"He loved to perform. He was the ultimate performer. I never heard him say an unkind word to anyone. You could bring anybody on the set, and he would sit and talk to them. He never set himself above anybody else, and he never made you feel like you had to treat him that way."

When you think back to that time, does any particular thought or comment stand out?
"I would say to myself, 'I'm working with Elvis Presley. Why aren't I in awe of him?' I kept thinking, 'That is Elvis Presley.' It never meant anything to me except that he was a terrific person to work with.

"It wasn't until many years later that I realized this, and my feelings for him haven't changed. I *did* work with the King. And if I didn't do anything else with my career, I got to kiss Elvis. I did it many times because we had many takes. He was just wonderful." ■

MAIN DISHES

*T*here was a time when it seemed all Elvis would eat was meat loaf and mashed potatoes with gravy. Then he began to eat Italian food. The hotel chef prepared the finest Italian dinners for him. Later, he went back to his usual hamburgers cooked extra well done with onions, relish, and mustard. ■

Hollywood Hamburgers

1¼ pounds ground beef
½ cup fine bread crumbs
¼ teaspoon mustard
½ cup ketchup
6 hamburger buns, buttered
2 tablespoons mayonnaise

Lettuce
Swiss cheese
Sweet pickle relish
1 tomato, sliced
1 small onion, sliced

In a medium bowl combine the ground beef, bread crumbs, mustard, and ketchup. Form into 6 patties, ½-inch thick. Melt enough butter in the bottom of a skillet just to coat. Brown the patties until thoroughly cooked. Split the buns and toast them lightly in the same skillet.

Spread a thin layer of mayonnaise on the buns. On one half place a leaf of the lettuce and a slice of the cheese. Place a patty on top of the cheese. Top with the relish, a slice of the tomato and the onion.

Makes 6 sandwiches.

Stuffed Hamburgers

6 slices bacon
1½ pounds ground beef
3 tablespoons chopped parsley
3 tablespoons chopped onion
1 teaspoon salt
¼ cup vegetable oil

1½ cups breadcrumbs
¼ teaspoon salt
¾ cup chopped cashews
Pepper to taste
Water
1 tomato, sliced

In a skillet fry the bacon until brown. Do not overcook. Drain on paper towels. Set aside.

In a medium bowl combine the ground beef, parsley, onion, salt, and oil. Mix to blend. In a separate bowl season the bread crumbs with ¼ teaspoon salt. Add the cashews and pepper. Add a few drops of the water to moisten slightly.

In a casserole dish with a cover alternately layer the meat mixture and the stuffing mixture, beginning with the meat and ending with the stuffing. Top with the tomato and bacon. Cover and bake at 350° for 45 minutes. Uncover and continue baking for 15 minutes more.

Makes 6 sandwiches.

Patty Melt

1 pound ground beef
¼ cup ketchup
½ cup bread crumbs
1 egg
Salt and pepper to taste

Butter
1 large onion, sliced
8 slices sourdough bread
4 slices American cheese

In a medium bowl mix the ground beef with the ketchup, bread crumbs, egg, salt, and pepper. Blend thoroughly. Shape into 4 patties. Set aside.

In a skillet melt enough butter just to coat the bottom. Sauté the onions until transparent. Set aside.

In the same skillet brown the patties until well done. Butter each slice of the bread on one side only. Place a slice of the bread, butter-side down, into the skillet. Layer with the hamburger patty, a slice of the cheese, and onions. Top with another slice of the bread, butter side up. Grill until the cheese has melted and the bread is somewhat toasted. Turn and toast the other side.

Makes 4 sandwiches.

Baked Meat Loaf

1 cup dry bread crumbs
1 cup milk
1½ pounds ground beef
½ pound ground pork
2 eggs, beaten
⅓ cup grated onion
¼ teaspoon salt

1 teaspoon pepper
½ teaspoon leaf sage
3 tablespoons packed light
  brown sugar
¼ cup ketchup
1 teaspoon dry mustard

In a small bowl soak the bread crumbs in the milk until mushy. In a medium bowl blend the beef with the pork, eggs, onion, salt, pepper, and sage. Blend in the bread crumb mixture and mix thoroughly. Form into a loaf. Place in a 9 x 13-inch baking pan. Set aside.

In a separate bowl blend the brown sugar, ketchup, and mustard. Mix thoroughly. Pour the mixture over the loaf. Bake at 350° for 1 hour and 45 minutes. Remove and let cool for 10 minutes.

Makes 6 servings.

Hawaiian Hamburgers

1 9-ounce can sliced pineapple
1 pound ground beef
Salt and pepper to taste
4 hamburger buns
2 tablespoons pineapple juice

¼ cup packed light brown
  sugar
½ cup ketchup
Liquid smoke

Drain the pineapple and reserve 2 tablespoons of the juice. In a medium bowl season the beef with the salt and pepper. Press a tablespoon of the meat into the center of each pineapple ring. Shape the remaining meat into 4 patties. In a separate bowl mix the pineapple juice, brown sugar, ketchup, and liquid smoke. Mix well. In a skillet pan-fry the patties until well done. Pan-fry the pineapple rings, making sure not to break the rings. Brush with the sauce while cooking. Place a patty on one side of each bun. Top each with a pineapple ring. Place the other half of each bun on top.

Makes 4 sandwiches.

Elvis enjoying the sights
while on location to film Blue Hawaii.

Sloppy Joe Burgers

2 tablespoons butter
½ cup chopped onion
1 pound ground beef
1 teaspoon mustard
1 10½-ounce can condensed
   tomato-rice soup

1 tablespoon steak sauce
⅓ cup water
Tabasco sauce
6 hamburger buns

In a skillet melt the butter. Sauté the onion until transparent. Drain and set aside.

Using the same skillet brown the ground beef. Drain. Add the onion, mustard, tomato-rice soup, steak sauce, and water. Season with the Tabasco sauce. Simmer until the water has cooked away. Serve on toasted hamburger buns.

Makes 6 sandwiches.

*K*itty Dolan recalled her date with Elvis. "Elvis was very considerate of other people. One night he took me to dinner at an elegant Hollywood nightclub. After an evening of music and singing, we'd go out for some sandwiches." ■

Bacon-Cheeseburgers

1 pound ground beef	Mustard
Salt and pepper	Ketchup
4 slices American cheese	1 onion, sliced
8 slices bacon	1 tomato, sliced
4 hamburger buns	Sweet pickle relish

Season the ground beef with the salt and pepper. Shape into 4 patties. In a skillet fry the patties until well done. Top each with a slice of the cheese. Continue cooking until the cheese has melted. Set aside in a warm oven.

In the same skillet fry the bacon until crisp. Drain and set aside.

Toast the hamburger buns. Spread with the mustard and ketchup. Place a patty on half of each bun and top with 2 bacon slices. Add the onion, tomatoes, and sweet pickle relish. Cover with the remaining halves of the hamburger buns.

Makes 4 sandwiches.

*B*eing generous was part of Elvis's charm. He didn't think he was better just because he had money. Quite the opposite. Elvis gave away so much because he had a kind heart. He didn't necessarily enjoy all the publicity that went along with his generous contributions. It embarrassed him.

While in Hollywood, he gave away truckloads of cars and jewelry to family and friends. He even bought homes for some of them. Once, Elvis bought a car for a woman who was admiring a model in a showroom. He could see that she had her heart set on owning the automobile. Every Christmas it was part of his tradition, along with a tree and turkey, to give away thousands of dollars to charities. ■

Elvis stayed at the Coco Palms Hotel while filming Blue Hawaii.

Country Fried Steak

1½ pounds flank steak,
   cut ½-inch thick
¾ cup all-purpose flour
¼ teaspoon pepper
½ teaspoon leaf basil
1 teaspoon salt
½ teaspoon leaf thyme

2 tablespoons butter
3 tablespoons butter
6 tablespoons all-purpose flour
1 teaspoon salt
¼ teaspoon pepper
3 cups milk

Pound the flank steak with a mallet until thin. In a medium bowl blend thoroughly the flour, pepper, basil, salt, and thyme. Dredge the steak in the flour mixture. In a heavy skillet melt 2 tablespoons butter until sizzling. Place the steak in the skillet and brown until well done. Place on a hot platter.

In a saucepan melt the remaining 3 tablespoons of butter. Blend in the flour, salt, and pepper. Slowly add the milk. Stir over medium heat until boiling. Cook to the desired thickness. If too thick add more milk. Top the steak with the gravy.

Makes 4 servings.

Swiss Steak

2 pounds round steak
⅓ cup all-purpose flour
Salt and pepper to taste
3 tablespoons shortening

1 onion, sliced
2 carrots, sliced
1½ cups stewed tomatoes

Cut the steak to 1-inch thickness. Wipe thoroughly with a cloth. Rub the steak with the flour, salt, and pepper. Pound the steak with a mallet. In a heavy skillet melt the shortening. Brown the meat on all sides. Add the onion, carrots, and tomatoes. Cover and simmer for 1½ hours or until the meat is tender.

Makes 6 servings.

Elvis and producer Hal Wallis on a Hawaiian beach.

Elvis with fans on location while filming Blue Hawaii.

Pepper Steak

⅓ cup all-purpose flour	1 tablespoon butter
¼ teaspoon salt	1 tablespoon all-purpose flour
⅛ teaspoon pepper	1 cup milk
4 beef steaks	Salt and pepper to taste
2 tablespoons butter	

In a medium bowl combine ⅓ cup flour with the salt and pepper. Dredge the steaks in the flour mixture. In a skillet melt 2 table-spoons of butter. Cook the steaks in the butter for 3 minutes, until brown on both sides. Add 1 tablespoon of butter to the pan drip-pings. Blend in 1 tablespoon of flour. Slowly blend in the milk, salt, and pepper, and cook until smooth. If thicker gravy is desired add more flour. Serve the gravy over the steaks.

Makes 4 servings.

Elvis and co-star Joan Blackman rehearsing a scene in Blue Hawaii.

Steak with Potatoes

1 pound potatoes
2 tablespoons red wine vinegar
2 garlic cloves, minced
3 tablespoons prepared mustard

1 teaspoon dry mustard
Salt and pepper to taste
2 sirloin steaks
2 tablespoons butter, melted

Line a broiler pan with aluminum foil. Set aside.

Wash and cut the potatoes in half. Place the potatoes in a saucepan of boiling salted water. Reduce the heat to medium. Cover and cook for 10 minutes.

In a medium bowl blend the vinegar with the garlic. Add the prepared mustard and the dry mustard. Season with salt and pepper to taste. Place the steaks on the prepared pan and brush with half of the mustard sauce. Drain the potatoes and toss with the melted butter. Arrange the potatoes around the steaks. Broil for 7 minutes. Turn the steaks and brush with the remaining mustard sauce. Broil for 11 minutes more. Pour the pan juices over the steaks.

Makes 2 servings.

Hawaiian Chicken

2 1½-pound whole fryer
  chickens
1½ teaspoons salt
Pepper to taste
4 slices white bread
1 cup light cream
¼ pound ground beef
½ pound ground veal
¼ cup minced onion

½ teaspoon ground ginger
½ cup sliced water chestnuts
2 tablespoons vegetable oil
1 cup sliced or chunk
  pineapple, drained
1 cup pineapple juice
2 tablespoons honey
½ cup sesame seeds

Oil a shallow baking pan and set it aside.

Wash the chickens thoroughly. Sprinkle with the salt and pepper. Remove the crusts from the sliced bread. In a medium bowl soak the bread in the cream. Squeeze out the excess liquid and mash together. In a separate bowl blend the ground beef and veal. Add the onion, ginger, and water chestnuts. Fold the meat mixture into the bread mixture. Stuff the chickens and close with skewers. In a skillet heat the oil and sauté the pineapple just until tender. Add the pineapple juice, honey, and sesame seeds and heat through. Set the pan aside.

Place the chickens in the prepared baking pan. Spoon some of the sauce over the chicken. Bake at 400° for 20 minutes. Reduce the heat to 350° and continue to bake another 35 minutes more. Turn the oven to 450° and cook for 5 minutes, until browned. Serve with sautéed pineapple.

Makes 4 servings.

*D*uring film breaks, Elvis liked to watch television in his dressing room. Sometimes he and his boys would get into a steady stream of horseplay around the studio, shooting at each other with water pistols or playing practical jokes on one another. At other times they would gather in a quiet corner of the studio and sing harmony together. ■

Parmesan Chicken

3 chicken breasts, split
½ cup freshly grated
  Parmesan cheese
Oil
1 garlic clove, minced
3 tablespoons all-purpose flour

1¾ cups chicken broth
½ cup sherry
1 4-ounce can mushrooms,
  drained
½ teaspoon salt
Pepper to taste

Wash the chicken thoroughly. Pat dry with paper towels. Rub the cheese over the chicken. In a skillet heat a small amount of oil and slowly brown the chicken. Remove the chicken and reserve the fat. In the same skillet add the garlic and cook until soft. Blend in the flour, broth, sherry, and mushrooms. Add the salt and season with the pepper. Return the chicken to the skillet. Cover and cook for 45 minutes or until the chicken is tender.

    Makes 6 servings.

Elvis helping set up a picnic.

*E*lvis's unusual taste in food delighted his fans. Elvis ate a breakfast of mashed potatoes, gravy, and hominy grits. Lunch consisted of more mashed potatoes, plus white bread topped with gravy. Dinner was a large steak. Like most Southerners, Elvis liked his meat cooked thoroughly. He also consumed large quantities of sodas and coffee. ■

Elvis and Joan Blackman waiting for their cues.

Fried Chicken

1 3-pound fryer chicken	1½ teaspoons paprika
Salt and pepper to taste	2 teaspoons salt
½ cup all-purpose flour	½ cup milk
½ cup bread crumbs	Shortening

Wash the frying chicken thoroughly and pat dry with paper towels. Sprinkle with the salt and pepper. In a medium bowl combine the flour, bread crumbs, and paprika. In a separate bowl blend the salt in the milk. Dip the chicken into the milk. Coat with the bread-crumb mixture. Place the chicken on a baking sheet and refrigerate for 1 hour.

In a skillet heat the shortening. Fry the chicken for 20 minutes or until golden. Place the chicken on a clean baking sheet. Bake at 350° for 30 minutes or until chicken is tender.

Makes 4 servings.

Chicken Baked in Cream

1 2-pound chicken
Salt and pepper to taste
4 tablespoons all-purpose flour
2 tablespoons cornmeal

½ cup oil
½ pound sliced mushrooms
3 cups milk

Wash and wipe dry the chicken. Cut the chicken into serving pieces. Sprinkle with the salt and pepper. Place the flour and the cornmeal into a paper bag, and shake to mix. Place pieces of chicken the bag and shake to coat. In a skillet heat the cooking oil. Brown the chicken. Place the chicken in a casserole dish.

In the same skillet sauté the mushrooms in the remaining oil, cooking over low heat until lightly browned. Add the leftover flour/cornmeal mixture. Slowly add the milk, stirring constantly. Stir over low heat until thick and smooth. Pour the sauce over the chicken. Bake at 325° for 1 hour or until the chicken is tender.

Makes 8 servings.

A confident Elvis delivering his lines.

Chicken Stew

1 4-pound stewing chicken,
   cut into serving pieces
⅓ cup all-purpose flour
2¼ teaspoons salt
⅓ cup fat (shortening)
3 cups water

4 medium tomatoes
2 onions
¼ teaspoon pepper
¼ cup water
1 tablespoon all-purpose flour

Wash and dry the chicken. In a medium bowl blend ⅓ cup flour with 1 teaspoon salt. Dredge the chicken into the flour mixture. In a skillet heat the fat and slowly brown the chicken. Add 3 cups of water and cover the skillet. Reduce the heat. Simmer for 1 hour.

Peel and slice the tomatoes and onion. Add the tomatoes and onion to the chicken with the remaining salt and pepper. Blend together ¼ cup of water and 1 tablespoon of flour. Stir the mixture into the pan liquid, blending well. Simmer until the chicken is tender.

Makes 6 servings.

Chicken & Rice

6 tablespoons butter
1 3-pound fryer chicken,
   cut into pieces
3 onions, sliced
2 green bell peppers, chopped
⅓ garlic clove, minced

1 16-ounce can tomatoes
1 10½-ounce can condensed
   chicken consommé
Salt and pepper to taste
1 cup uncooked rice
1 9-ounce package peas

In a skillet melt 3 tablespoons of butter and sauté the chicken until brown. In a separate skillet melt the remaining butter. Sauté the onion, green bell pepper, and garlic. Add the tomatoes. Mix in the chicken consommé, salt, pepper, and rice. Cover the skillet and let it cook for 20 minutes over low heat. Add the peas and cook for 5 minutes more.

Place the chicken in a casserole dish. Pour the rice mixture over the chicken. Cover and bake at 350° for 25 minutes or until the chicken is tender.

Makes 6 servings.

Chicken Pie

5 tablespoons butter
½ cup sliced onion
¼ cup all-purpose flour
2 cups chicken stock
Salt
Pepper
3 cups chopped cooked chicken
1 cup canned peas

1 cup cooked diced carrots
2 cups all-purpose flour
2 teaspoons baking powder
1 teaspoon salt
½ cup butter
1 egg, slightly beaten
¼ cup milk

In a skillet melt the butter and sauté the onion. Cook until the onion is transparent. Add the flour. Stir until well blended. Gradually add the chicken stock, and cook until smooth and thick. Season with the salt and pepper. In a large casserole dish arrange the chicken with the vegetables. Cover with the sauce and set aside.

In a medium bowl sift the flour. Remeasure 2 cups of flour and resift with the baking powder and 1 teaspoon of salt. Cut in the butter with a pastry blender. Add the egg. Add just enough milk to make a soft dough. Turn the dough onto a floured board and knead for 30 seconds. Turn and roll to ½-inch thick. Cut with a floured biscuit cutter. Place the biscuits on top of the chicken. Brush with milk. Bake at 400° for 30 minutes.

Makes 5 servings.

Trying to stay warm after a swim in the Pacific Ocean.

Elvis with Marlyn Mason, his co-star in The Trouble with Girls.

Chicken Spoon Bread

1 cup cold water	1½ teaspoons salt
1 cup cornmeal	1 teaspoon baking powder
3 cups boiling water	1 tablespoon butter
1 teaspoon salt	1 cup chopped cooked chicken
3 egg yolks, beaten	3 egg whites

Grease a 1-quart casserole dish and set it aside.

In the top of a double boiler over simmering water add 1 cup cold water to the cornmeal. Add the boiling water and 1 teaspoon salt. Cook, stirring constantly, until the mixture begins to boil. Cover and cook over boiling water for 30 minutes, stirring occasionally.

In a medium bowl combine the cornmeal mixture and the egg yolks. Add 1½ teaspoons of salt, the baking powder, and butter. Mix thoroughly. Add the chicken. Stir to coat the chicken. Beat the egg whites until stiff but not dry. Fold the egg whites into the chicken mixture. Turn into the prepared casserole dish. Bake at 325° for 1 hour.

Makes 6 servings.

*P*eople didn't realize how shy Elvis really was. During his first few months on the movie set, he didn't know whether he could eat lunch in the commissary with the other stars. ■

Elvis demonstrates his affinity for cars, even on location.

*E*lvis basically liked home-cooked meals. His mother's southern cooking spoiled him, but while living in Hollywood nothing pleased him more than plenty of cheeseburgers and French fries and a couple of chocolate shakes. At the hotel he ate pork chops and mashed potatoes with gravy. The chef would prepare these foods especially for Elvis, including apple pie with vanilla ice cream for dessert. ■

Baked Chicken

1 3-pound fryer chicken, cut into pieces	¾ teaspoon salt
1 cup all-purpose flour	¼ teaspoon pepper
1 teaspoon curry powder	¼ cup butter
	½ cup chicken consommé

In a medium bowl sift the flour. Add the curry powder, salt, and pepper. Dredge the chicken in the flour mixture. In a skillet melt the butter and brown the chicken evenly. Place the chicken in a 2-quart casserole dish. Pour the remaining butter and the chicken consommé over the chicken. Bake at 350° for 25 minutes or until the chicken is tender.
Makes 6 servings.

*D*uring one break in the filming schedule, Elvis announced he was hungry. It was already past lunchtime, and so he asked his boys to join him back at the hotel for some bacon and tomato sandwiches. ■

Lemon Chicken

2 2-pound fryer chickens	½ teaspoon pepper
2 lemons	2 teaspoons sugar
Butter	1 teaspoon paprika
2 teaspoons salt	

Cut the chickens in half. Cut the lemons in half and rub the outside of each chicken. In a saucepan melt the butter. Coat the chickens in the melted butter. In a medium bowl mix the salt with the pepper, sugar, and paprika. Blend thoroughly. Dredge the chicken in the spice mixture.

Place the chicken in a broiler pan. Place the pan 8 inches away from the heat. Broil slowly. The chicken should begin to brown after 12 minutes. Turn when the chicken is browned. Baste with melted butter and continue broiling until the chicken is thoroughly done.

Makes 4 servings.

*O*n Elvis's first day on the set, he was approached by producer David Weisbart who wanted to discuss the possibility of casting him as the lead in the movie *The James Dean Story*. James Dean had died in 1955, and in 1956 Hollywood already was considering a feature film on his life. Elvis said he was flattered to be considered for the role. ■

Chicken Cacciatore

1 frying chicken	½ cup olive oil
3 tablespoons butter	2 garlic cloves
1 chopped onion	3½ cups tomatoes
½ pound sliced mushrooms	Chopped parsley
½ cup all-purpose flour	1 teaspoon leaf oregano
1 teaspoon salt	1 teaspoon salt
¼ teaspoon pepper	½ teaspoon pepper

Wash the chicken thoroughly. Dry with paper towels. Cut into serving pieces and set aside.

In a skillet melt the butter and sauté the onion and mushrooms until the onion is transparent. In a medium bowl sift the flour with the 1 teaspoon of salt and ¼ teaspoon of pepper. Dredge the chicken into the coating mixture.

In a skillet heat the olive oil and sauté the garlic until light brown. Place the chicken skin-side down in the skillet. Brown on all sides.

In a separate bowl blend the tomatoes, parsley, oregano, 1 teaspoon of salt, and ½ teaspoon of pepper. Add the tomato mixture to the browned chicken along with the mushrooms and onion. Cover and cook over low heat for 30 minutes.

Makes 4 servings.

Chicken Croquettes

3 tablespoons butter
1 tablespoon chopped onion
1 cup sliced mushrooms
¼ cup all-purpose flour
1 cup milk
Salt and pepper to taste
2 cups diced cooked chicken

½ cup bread crumbs
2 eggs, beaten
¼ cup butter
¼ cup all-purpose flour
1 teaspoon salt
⅛ teaspoon pepper
2 cups milk

In a skillet melt 3 tablespoons of butter and sauté the onion and mushrooms until the onion is transparent. Add the flour and blend until smooth. Slowly stir in the milk, and season with salt and pepper. Add the chicken and mix thoroughly. Refrigerate until well chilled.

Shape into croquettes. In a medium bowl blend the bread crumbs with the eggs. Dip the croquettes into the egg batter. Fry in hot oil for 3 minutes or until brown. Drain on paper towels.

In a saucepan melt ¼ cup of butter over low heat. Add the flour, salt, and pepper, and stir until well blended. Slowly stir in the milk. Cook until thick and smooth. Pour the gravy over croquettes.

Makes 2 servings.

Elvis getting instructions from Hal Wallis
for a scene.

Elvis playing with a Welsh corgi on the set of Blue Hawaii.

*"E*lvis's neighbors were the people who drove trucks, worked in gas stations, and spent their youth in roadside taverns listening to tales of their heartbreak hotel. Their life was an Elvis song." —Robert Cary, *The Commercial Appeal* ■

Hawaiian Ham

4 tablespoons butter
½ chopped green bell pepper
2 cups diced cooked ham
1 8-ounce can crushed pineapple
2 tablespoons packed light
  brown sugar

1½ teaspoons cornstarch
1½ teaspoons vinegar
1½ teaspoons mustard
Salt and pepper to taste
¾ cup cold water
1⅓ cups cooked white rice

In a skillet melt 2 tablespoons of butter. Sauté the green bell pepper and ham for 4 minutes. Drain the crushed pineapple and reserve the liquid. In a medium bowl combine the pineapple juice, brown sugar, cornstarch, vinegar, mustard, salt, and pepper. Add the water and blend thoroughly. Add the mixture to the ham mixture along with the crushed pineapple. Bring to a boil, stirring constantly.

Cook the rice according to the package directions, adding 2 tablespoons of butter. To serve, spoon the ham mixture over the rice.

Makes 4 servings.

Barbecued Chicken

2 fryer chickens, cut in half
1 tablespoon molasses
1 teaspoon dry mustard
2 teaspoons Worcestershire
  sauce

⅓ cup melted butter
1 teaspoon salt
¼ teaspoon pepper
2 tablespoons vinegar

Wash the chickens thoroughly. Pat dry with paper towels. Place the chickens on a broiler rack, skin-side down. In a medium bowl blend the molasses with the mustard, Worcestershire sauce, salt, pepper, butter, and vinegar. Blend until smooth.

Brush the chicken thoroughly with the marinade. Broil for 30 minutes. Baste the chicken with marinade during the cooking process. Turn the chicken, baste, and broil for 5 minutes. Baste once again, turn the chicken, and continue broiling until the chicken is thoroughly cooked.

Makes 4 servings.

*E*lvis liked to spend an evening with a date driving around Hollywood and taking in the sights of the city. ■

Stuffed Chicken

3 tablespoons butter
¼ cup chopped celery
1 chopped onion
3 cups breadcrumbs
½ teaspoon salt
⅛ teaspoon pepper
½ teaspoon leaf thyme
2 tablespoons parsley
1 4-pound roasting chicken
¼ cup butter

1 cup water
6 potatoes, peeled and sliced
6 chopped carrots
1 onion, peeled
2 teaspoons salt
¼ teaspoon pepper
3 tablespoons all-purpose flour
3 tablespoons drippings
1 cup chicken stock
1 cup light cream

In a skillet melt the butter and sauté the onion and celery in butter until golden. Remove the pan from the heat. Add the bread crumbs, salt, pepper, thyme, and parsley, and toss with a fork to coat.

Wash the chicken thoroughly. Pat dry with paper towels. Place the stuffing mixture inside the chicken. In a deep skillet melt ¼ cup of butter. Place the chicken in the pan and brown on all sides. Add the water and cover. Simmer for 35 minutes. Add the potatoes, carrots, and onion. Season with the salt and pepper. Cover and continue cooking for 30 minutes more or until the vegetables are tender.

In a saucepan blend the flour into the drippings. Cook over low heat, stirring constantly. Add the chicken stock and light cream, and cook until thick. Additional flour may be added for the desired thickness. Serve with vegetables and chicken.

Makes 6 servings.

*I*t was not unusual for Elvis to drive to an out-of-the-way café where he and his date would enjoy hot dogs and hamburgers and play records on the jukebox. ■

Pork Roast

1 5-pound pork shoulder	¼ teaspoon pepper
Salt and pepper	½ teaspoon oregano
4 cups bread crumbs	⅓ cup butter, melted
1 cup diced celery	1 teaspoon salt
¼ cup chopped scallions	Fresh lemon juice

Remove the bone from the pork shoulder. Make a pocket for the stuffing. Season the pork with the salt and pepper.

In a medium bowl combine the bread crumbs, celery, scallions, pepper, oregano, butter, and salt. Blend thoroughly. Add a little of the fresh lemon juice. Stuff the pocket with the mixture.

Tie the roast with a string. Place the meat, fat-side up, in an open roasting pan. Score the meat with a sharp knife. Bake at 325° for 3 hours and 30 minutes. Serve with gravy made from the pan drippings.

Makes 8 servings.

Elvis enjoying a picnic lunch with the cast and crew.

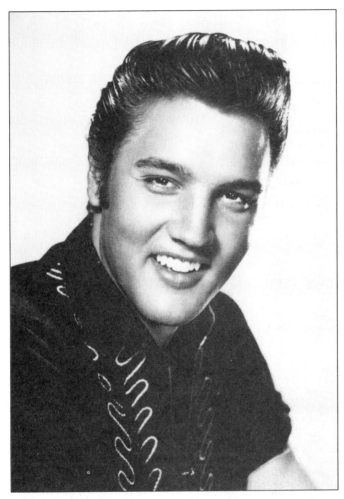

Pictures like this adorned the covers of movie magazines.

*F*ilms Elvis had an interest in making or was offered to make but never did:

*Your Cheatin' Heart, Midnight Cowboy, A Star Is Born,
The James Dean Story, How the West Was Won, West Side Story,
The Rainmaker, Thunder Road,* and *Sweet Bird of Youth.* ∎

Ham with Pineapple Sauce

1½-pound ham slice,
  ¾-inch thick
1 21-ounce can pineapple chunks,
  drained and juice reserved
1 tablespoon cornstarch
1 tablespoon all-purpose flour
2 tablespoons butter

2 tablespoons packed light
  brown sugar
1 tablespoon vinegar
¼ teaspoon ground ginger
¼ teaspoon ground allspice
¼ cup chopped green bell
  pepper

In a large skillet brown the ham on both sides. Place the ham on a serving platter. In a saucepan combine the pineapple juice, the cornstarch, and flour. Cook over medium heat until smooth. Add the butter, sugar, vinegar, ginger, allspice, and green bell pepper. Heat for 2 minutes. Add 1 cup of pineapple chunks and cook until the sauce is thick. Pour the sauce over the ham slice.
Makes 4 servings.

Baked Pork Chops

2 tablespoons melted butter
1½ cups bread crumbs
2 tablespoons grated Parmesan
  cheese
¼ teaspoon salt

½ teaspoon leaf oregano
¼ teaspoon pepper
1 egg, beaten
2 tablespoons milk
6 pork chops

Coat the bottom of a 13 x 9-inch baking pan with the melted butter. Set it aside.

In a medium bowl blend the bread crumbs, Parmesan cheese, salt, oregano, and pepper. Mix thoroughly. In a separate bowl blend the egg with the milk. Dredge the pork chops in the bread crumb mixture. Dip the chops into the egg mixture and again into the bread crumb mixture. Arrange the chops in the prepared pan. Bake at 325° for 30 minutes. Turn the pork chops and continue baking for 30 minutes more.
Makes 6 servings.

Pork & Sauerkraut Casserole

1 pound pork sausage	2½ cups sauerkraut
2 tablespoons fat	¼ cup pineapple juice
1 14-ounce can pineapple chunks	1 tablespoon packed light
1 apple, sliced	brown sugar

In a skillet cook the sausage over low heat for 15 minutes, browning thoroughly. Drain all but 2 tablespoons fat. Add the pineapple chunks and apple to the sausage. Continue to cook for 5 minutes more. Add the sauerkraut and pineapple juice. Sprinkle the brown sugar on top. Cover. Cook over low heat for 40 minutes.

Makes 4 servings.

Elvis with cast and crew on the set of Frankie *and* Johnny.

With fans in Hawaii.

Ham & Pork Loaf

⅓ cup vinegar
⅔ cup packed light brown
  sugar
1 cup water
1 teaspoon dry mustard
Salt and pepper to taste
1½ tablespoons cornstarch
1 pound ground ham

1½ pounds ground pork
2 eggs, beaten
1 cup bread crumbs
1 cup milk
1 chopped onion
1 teaspoon dry mustard
1 tablespoon chopped parsley
Salt and pepper to taste

In a saucepan combine the vinegar, brown sugar, water, mustard, salt, and pepper. Bring the mixture to a boil. Add the cornstarch mixed with a little cold water. Cook over low heat, stirring constantly, until the sauce becomes thick and smooth.

In a medium bowl combine the ham and pork. Add the eggs, bread crumbs, milk, onion, mustard, and parsley. Season with salt and pepper and blend thoroughly. Place the mixture in a loaf pan. Bake at 350° for 1 hour and 45 minutes. Top with sauce.

Makes 6 servings.

*W*hen Elvis dated, there was never a huge fanfare. "When I go out, I usually don't go anywhere," he explained. "We just ride around in my car, have dinner in my apartment, or go to a late movie." ∎

Country Fried Pork Chops

6 pork chops
2 tablespoons milk
2 eggs, beaten
½ teaspoon salt
1 cup bread crumbs
Pepper to taste
Butter

¼ cup water
3 tablespoons butter
6 tablespoon all-purpose flour
1 teaspoon salt
¼ teaspoon pepper
3 cups milk

With a mallet pound the pork chops to ½-inch thickness. In a medium bowl blend the milk and eggs. In a separate bowl mix the salt, bread crumbs, and pepper. Dip the pork chops in the egg mixture. Dredge them in the crumb mixture. In a skillet melt some butter and brown the pork chops on both sides. Add the water. Cover and cook over low heat for 45 minutes. Make sure the pork chops do not stick to the skillet.

In a saucepan melt 3 tablespoons of butter. Blend in the flour, salt, and pepper. Slowly add the milk. Stir over medium heat until boiling. Cook to the desired thickness. If too thick add more milk. Top the pork chops with the gravy.

Makes 6 servings.

*E*lvis admitted he loved fried bananas, browning them in butter and brown sugar. Sometimes for a change he would eat peanut butter sandwiches with marshmallow cream. Fried chicken was always on the top of his list along with grits, eggs, and plenty of crisp bacon. ∎

Elvis relaxing on the water, waiting for the next scene.

Pork Sausage & Sauerkraut

1½ pounds pork sausage	1 chopped onion
3 tablespoons parsley	Salt and pepper to taste
1 tablespoon chopped green bell pepper	3 cups sauerkraut

In a medium bowl blend the pork sausage with the parsley, green bell pepper, and onion. Mix thoroughly. Season with salt and pepper. In a skillet fry the crumbled sausage over low heat until thoroughly cooked. Drain on paper towels.

Place the sauerkraut in a casserole dish. Top with the sausage. Cover and bake at 300° for 10 minutes or until the sauerkraut is thoroughly heated.

Makes 4 servings.

Sausage Pizza

1 envelope dry active yeast
1 cup warm water (110°)
4 cups all-purpose flour
2 teaspoons sugar
1½ teaspoons salt
1 tablespoon butter
1 egg white
Vegetable oil

¾ pound pork sausage
6 tomatoes, sliced
Sweet basil to taste
2 ounces Romano cheese, grated
½ cup onion, chopped
¾ teaspoon leaf oregano
Salt and pepper to taste

In a small bowl dissolve the yeast in ¼ cup warm water. Set aside for 10 minutes.

In a medium bowl sift the flour. Remeasure 4 cups of flour. Place the remaining water in a large bowl. Add the sugar, salt, butter, and 1 cup of flour. Beat until smooth. Add the yeast mixture and the egg white, and blend until thoroughly mixed. Add the remaining flour. Beat to make a stiff dough. Turn the dough out onto a floured board and knead for 10 minutes until smooth. Place the dough in a greased bowl, then turn it greased side up. Cover and let rise for 1 hour, until the dough has doubled in bulk. Knead again.

Place the dough on a floured board and cut it into quarters. Cover with the greased bowl. Let the dough stand for 10 minutes. Roll each piece into an 8-inch circle. Place in 4 separate pie tins. Press until ¼-inch thick on the bottom and slightly thicker on the sides. Brush with the vegetable oil.

In a skillet pan-fry the pork sausage until slightly brown. Do not over cook. Drain. Spread sliced tomatoes over the bottom of each crust. Sprinkle sweet basil over the tomatoes. Add half of the grated Romano cheese and all of the partially cooked pork sausage. Top with the onion and the remaining Romano cheese. Season with the oregano and the salt and pepper. Bake at 450° for 20 minutes or until the crust is done.

Makes 4 servings.

Lasagna

2 tablespoons olive oil
1 garlic clove, chopped
⅓ cup chopped celery
½ pound ground beef
2 cups canned tomatoes
3 tablespoons tomato paste
1 teaspoon salt
¼ teaspoon leaf oregano

Pepper to taste
2 quarts water
2 teaspoons salt
7 ounces lasagna noodles
¼ pound mozzarella cheese
¾ cup ricotta cheese
⅓ cup grated Parmesan cheese

Grease a 10 x 6-inch baking pan and set it aside.

In a 3-quart saucepan heat the olive oil. Add the garlic and celery and sauté until tender. Add the ground beef and cook until brown. Add the canned tomatoes, tomato paste, salt, oregano, and pepper. Stir to blend. Cover and simmer for 1 hour.

In a soup pot heat the water to boiling. Add the salt and noodles. Cook for 7 minutes until the noodles are tender. Drain. In a medium bowl dice the mozzarella cheese. Place ¼ of the sauce in the bottom of the prepared baking pan. Spread evenly. Add ⅓ of the noodles. Sprinkle with the diced mozzarella. Add another layer of the noodles and ricotta cheese. Add ¼ more of the sauce. Top with the remaining noodles. Sprinkle with the Parmesan cheese. Bake at 375° for 45 minutes or until done. Serve with the remaining sauce poured over the top.

Makes 4 servings.

Elvis at work filming Blue Hawaii.

Macaroni & Cheese

4½ tablespoons butter
3 tablespoons all-purpose flour
1½ teaspoons salt
Pepper to taste
3 cups milk
1 8-ounce package macaroni

½ pound grated Cheddar
   cheese
1 tablespoon minced onion
Mustard
Worcestershire sauce
½ cup buttered crumbs

In a saucepan melt the butter over low heat. Add the flour, salt, and pepper. Blend thoroughly. Remove from heat. Add the milk and return to heat. Cook, stirring constantly, until thick and smooth.

In a large saucepan cook the macaroni according to the package directions. Rinse and drain. In a large bowl combine the macaroni with the sauce, grated cheese, onion, mustard to taste, and Worcestershire sauce to taste. Pour into a large casserole dish. Top with the buttered crumbs. Bake at 375° for 25 minutes or until brown on top.

Makes 6 servings.

On the set of Loving You.

Elvis with Hal Wallis and guests.

Scrambled Eggs with Bacon

8 slices bacon cut in half
8 eggs
¼ cup milk
1 chopped onion

¼ teaspoon salt
¼ teaspoon pepper
1 cup grated Cheddar cheese

In a skillet fry the bacon until crisp. Drain the bacon on paper towels and set aside.

In a medium bowl beat the eggs with the milk. Add the onion, salt, and pepper. Pour the egg mixture into the skillet used to fry the bacon. Scramble until hard. Add the bacon right before the eggs are done. Before serving sprinkle cheese over the eggs.

Makes 4 servings.

Spinach with Bacon and Eggs

1½ pounds fresh spinach
1¼ cups boiling water
8 slices bacon

3 hard-boiled eggs, sliced
Salt and pepper to taste

Wash the spinach under running water. Pat dry with paper towels. In a saucepan place the spinach into already boiling water. Boil for 5 minutes until tender. Drain thoroughly. In a skillet fry the bacon until crisp. Drain on paper towels. Reserve the bacon drippings.

In a medium bowl toss the spinach with enough bacon drippings to coat. Season with the salt and pepper. Place the spinach on a platter and serve with the hard-boiled eggs and strips of cooked bacon.

Makes 4 servings.

Eggs Benedict

4 eggs
½ teaspoon salt
4 slices ham
2 English muffins, split
¼ cup butter

¼ cup cream
2 egg yolks
1 tablespoon fresh lemon juice
Salt and pepper to taste

Fill a skillet with straight sides ⅔ full of water. Add the salt. Bring to a rolling boil, then reduce the heat. Break the eggs into the water and poach until the desired firmness. In a separate skillet pan-fry the ham until lightly browned. Toast the muffins.

Melt the butter in the top of a double boiler over simmering water. Add the cream and egg yolks. Mix thoroughly so the eggs are well blended. Add the lemon juice, salt, and pepper. Continue stirring over hot water until thick and smooth.

Place a slice of ham on top of a muffin. Top with a poached egg. Pour the sauce on top of the egg. Serve immediately.

Makes 4 servings.

A classic publicity pose.

*E*lvis and his boys lived quietly in two large suites at the
Beverly Wilshire Hotel with nary a breath of gags or weekend
parties. Every working morning at 6:30, a blast of rock 'n' roll music
would burst from the clock radio, and Elvis would reach over and
turn down the volume while ordering his usual breakfast of cereal,
bananas, and milk.

"Lots of milk, Miss. Maybe two quarts," Elvis would say to the room service operator.

At 7:30 in the evening after viewing the daily rushes, he and his pals [Gene and Carrol Smith] headed back to the hotel. Supper, as Elvis called it, usually consisted of French-fried potatoes, sliced tomatoes, and bacon. These ingredients were folded together into sort of a huge Dagwood sandwich and consumed with two quarts of milk.

After dinner, records were played while Elvis sang. His friends would shoot some pool on the pool table he had ordered installed in their suite. At 9:00 P.M., Elvis began to study the next day's scenes. Later he would work on characterization. He was in bed at 11:00 P.M.

Relaxation outside the hotel suite proved a problem because fans constantly lurked at every hotel exit and hounded him for his autograph. Many fans insisted on following him everywhere. On Sundays, though, Elvis and his friends sometimes managed to walk the two short blocks to the Beverly Theater to see a movie. And on Saturday evenings a pretty girl or two would be asked to join him for supper and music. ■

Fried Tomato Sandwiches

4 medium tomatoes
1 cup cottage cheese
1 tablespoon chopped chives
¼ teaspoon salt

2 eggs, beaten
1 tablespoon milk
1 cup fine cracker crumbs
¼ cup butter

Wash and peel the tomatoes. Cut each crosswise into 4 slices. Set aside.

In a medium bowl blend the cottage cheese with the chives and salt. Spread the cottage cheese mixture over half the tomato slices. Top with the remaining tomato slices. In a separate bowl combine the eggs and milk. Dip the tomatoes into the egg mixture. Dredge in the cracker crumbs. In a large skillet melt the butter and fry the breaded tomatoes on both sides for 5 minutes until golden. Serve hot.

Makes 4 sandwiches.

Bacon & Tomato Club Sandwiches

15 slices white bread	Lettuce
10 slices bacon	½ cup mayonnaise
6 medium tomatoes	

Toast the bread on both sides and spread lightly with butter. In a skillet fry the bacon until crisp. Drain on paper towels. Slice the tomatoes thinly. Place lettuce leaves on 5 slices of the toasted bread. Place bacon and tomato on top of the lettuce. Place 5 more slices of bread on top of the tomatoes. Spread mayonnaise. Repeat layering with lettuce, tomato, and bacon. Top with remaining bread.

Makes 5 sandwiches.

Lunchtime for Elvis sometimes was a light snack of crackers, yogurt, and a large glass of milk. ■

Grilled Ham & Cheese Sandwiches

3 tablespoons butter	4 slices American cheese
8 slices white bread	½ pound thinly sliced cooked
Butter	ham

In a skillet melt 3 tablespoons of butter. Spread butter on one side of each slice of bread. On the unbuttered side of the bread place a slice of the cheese and some of the ham. Top with another slice of the bread, butter-side out. Place the sandwiches in the skillet. Cook until the cheese has melted and the bread becomes toasted.

Makes 4 sandwiches.

With Angela Lansbury in Blue Hawaii.

*O*ne day on the set, Elvis noticed that it was lunchtime. He had been talking to a pretty young fan who was allowed to watch the filming that day, and so he leaned over and said, "I'm getting hungry. Would you like to join me for a sandwich I have already ordered?" With that they proceeded to his dressing room. There, ready for Elvis, was a platter of bacon and tomato sandwiches and tall glasses of ice-cold Pepsi. ∎

Chili Cheese Dogs

1 pound kidney beans
1 clove garlic
2 teaspoons chili powder
1 onion, chopped
¼ pound bacon, chopped
4 cups water

1 16-ounce can tomatoes,
  drained
½ teaspoon salt
6 bun-length hot dogs
6 slices American cheese
6 hot dog buns

Wash the beans. Cover with water and let soak overnight.

Drain the beans and place them in a soup pot with the garlic, chili powder, onion, and bacon. Add the water. Simmer for 4 hours, until the beans are tender. Add the tomatoes the last hour of cooking.

In a saucepan boil the hot dogs for 8 minutes. Drain. Fold the cheese into the hot dog buns. Place the hot dogs on top of the cheese. Pour the chili over the hot dogs. Place in a baking pan. Bake at 325° until the cheese has melted.

Makes 6 servings.

Ham & Egg Sandwiches

4 hard-boiled eggs
½ cup mayonnaise
½ pound ground cooked ham
½ teaspoon mustard
¼ cup chopped sweet pickle

¼ teaspoon salt
1 teaspoon vinegar
1 teaspoon chopped onion
10 slices white bread
Lettuce

In a medium bowl mash the eggs with the back of a fork. Add the mayonnaise and ham, and blend until smooth. Add the mustard, sweet pickle, salt, vinegar, and onion. Mix thoroughly. Butter one side of each slice of the white bread. Spread about ¼ cup of filling on each of 5 slices of bread. Top each sandwich with lettuce and a slice of bread.

Makes 5 sandwiches.

Elvis on the set of Girls! Girls! Girls!

*M*ary Jenkins, one of Elvis's cooks, reports that his favorite birthday dinner was "A six-pound roast cooked four hours at 350 degrees, creamed potatoes with butter, mixed vegetables (peas, beans, corn, and carrots with butter and salt), crowder peas with salt pork, and cornbread made with eggs, milk, and shortening. For dessert he liked banana pudding with eight eggs, six cups of milk, two and one-half cups of sugar and a one-fourth pound of butter." Also included was a large box of vanilla wafers and, of course, bananas. ■

Grilled Sausage Sandwiches

1 pound pork sausage	8 slices sourdough bread
Salt and pepper to taste	8 slices mozzarella cheese
1 onion, sliced	4 tablespoons butter
1 green bell pepper, sliced	

In a medium bowl blend the sausage with the salt and pepper. Shape into 4 patties. In a skillet cook the sausage patties for 12 minutes, or until brown. Add the onion and green bell pepper and cook until the vegetables are tender. Remove the patties and vegetables and drain the fat from the skillet. Place a sausage patty on a slice of the sourdough bread. Add the cheese and vegetables. Top with slice of the sourdough bread. Repeat for the remaining sandwiches. Using the same skillet melt the butter. Place the assembled sandwiches in the skillet and grill until the cheese has melted.

Makes 4 sandwiches.

Grilled Turkey Sandwiches

1 pound ground turkey	8 slices sourdough bread
2 tablespoons lime juice	1 avocado, sliced
1 tablespoon olive oil	4 slices Cheddar cheese
Salt and pepper to taste	Lettuce
⅓ cup mayonnaise	

Line a baking pan with aluminum foil. Set aside.

In a medium bowl place the ground turkey with the lime juice, olive oil, and salt and pepper. Blend thoroughly. Form the ground turkey into 4 patties. Place on the prepared pan. Broil for 6 minutes, turning once. Make sure both sides are evenly browned.

Spread an even layer of the mayonnaise on each slice of the bread. Place a patty in between the bread with avocado slices and a slice of the cheese. Return to the broiler. Broil another 30 seconds or until the bread is toasted. Garnish with lettuce.

Makes 4 servings.

Broiled Ham Sandwiches

1½ cups condensed tomato soup	2 egg yolks, beaten
½ pound grated American cheese	2 tablespoons horseradish
	8 slices sourdough bread
	8 slices cooked ham

Line a baking sheet with aluminum foil. Set aside.

In a saucepan simmer the soup until thick and smooth. Add the grated cheese. Stir until the cheese has melted. Add the beaten egg yolks. Continue cooking for 1 minute, until the soup is smooth and well blended. Remove the pan from the heat. Add the horseradish. Set aside to cool.

Spread 4 slices of bread with soup/cheese mixture. Top with the slices of cooked ham. Top with the other 4 slices of bread. Place the ham sandwiches on prepared baking sheet. Broil until the ham is brown and becomes crispy.

Makes 4 sandwiches.

*O*n many occasions Elvis and his boys would run in and around the studio offices shooting each other with water pistols. ■

Corned Beef Sandwiches

1 cup chopped corned beef	½ cup chopped celery
1 teaspoon minced onion	1 tablespoon mustard
2 tablespoons mayonnaise	4 slices white bread

In a medium bowl combine the corned beef, onion, mayonnaise, celery, and mustard. Mix thoroughly. Toast the sliced bread. Spread with butter. Mound the corned beef mixture between slices of toasted bread.

Makes 2 sandwiches.

*W*hile living in Hollywood, Elvis found it difficult to go to public theaters, so he would hold private screenings in his hotel suite. Said to be among his favorite films were *To Kill a Mockingbird, Rebel Without a Cause, The Godfather, Patton,* and *The Party.* ■

Turkey Loaf Sandwiches

3 cups chopped cooked turkey	1 loaf sliced white bread
1 cup chopped celery	½ cup butter
½ teaspoon grated onion	1 tablespoon milk
1 cup mayonnaise	⅔ cup crumbled blue cheese
Salt and pepper to taste	3 ounces cream cheese

In a medium bowl blend together the cooked turkey, celery, onion, and mayonnaise. Season with the salt and pepper. Trim the crusts from the bread. Place 3 slices of bread on a baking sheet. Butter the slices. Spread with the turkey mixture. Butter 3 more slices of the bread and spread them with the turkey mixture. Place one on each stack. Continue this pattern until each stack holds 6 slices of bread for a total of 18 slices. Press each stack firmly together.

In a separate bowl blend the milk with the blue cheese and cream cheese. Mix until smooth. Spread the cheese mixture over the tops and sides of each stack. Refrigerate overnight. To serve slice each stack in half.

Makes 6 servings.

*E*lvis and Joan O'Brien, his co-star in *It Happened at the World's Fair,* were spotted having lunch together at the top of the World's Fair Space Needle. They dined on shrimp salads and French bread. ■

Elvis on the set of Girls! Girls! Girls!

Poorboy Sandwiches

¼ cup mayonnaise	8 slices American cheese
2 tablespoons sour cream	1 pound sliced cooked ham
2 dill pickles, chopped	3 tomatoes, sliced
4 oblong hard rolls, split	¼ cup minced onion
Lettuce	Salt and pepper to taste

In a medium bowl blend the mayonnaise, sour cream, and dill pickles. Spread on both halves of the rolls. Cover the bottom half of each roll with a leaf of lettuce and 2 slices of American cheese. Add slices of the ham and tomato on top of the cheese. Sprinkle with the onions. Season with the salt and pepper. Top each with the other half of the roll.

Makes 4 sandwiches.

*E*lvis shot *Flaming Star* for 20th Century Fox in exactly forty-two days. Most of it was filmed at the studio in Los Angeles, but for some of the location shots Elvis had to travel to the sprawling Conejo Ranch in the San Fernando Valley. ■

Barbecued Lamb Sandwiches

1 pound ground lamb	2 tablespoons chopped parsley
¼ teaspoon curry powder	3 tablespoons fresh lemon juice
½ teaspoon garlic salt	Salt and pepper to taste
½ cup water	6 hard rolls, split
6 ounces tomato paste	¼ cup mayonnaise
2 tablespoons packed light brown sugar	

In a skillet brown the lamb in the curry powder and garlic salt. Add the water. In a medium bowl blend the tomato paste, brown sugar, parsley, lemon juice, salt, and pepper. Mix thoroughly. Add the tomato mixture to the lamb. Simmer uncovered for 4 minutes. Spread both halves of the rolls with the mayonnaise. Fill each roll with lamb mixture.

Makes 6 sandwiches.

---

*E*lvis briefly dated Connie Stevens while making *Kid Galahad*. He shot the film on location in Idlewild, California. ∎

Peanut Butter & Banana Sandwiches

¼ cup creamy peanut butter	10 slices buttered bread
2 very ripe bananas, peeled and mashed	Butter

In a medium bowl blend the peanut butter with the banana until creamy. Spread the mixture over 5 slices of bread. Top with the remaining bread.

In a skillet melt enough butter to coat the bottom of the pan. Place the sandwiches in the butter and fry them until the bread is lightly toasted. Flip to fry the other side. Drain on paper towels.

Makes 5 sandwiches.

Double-Decker Egg Salad Sandwiches

⅓ cup mayonnaise
8 hard-boiled eggs, chopped
2 tablespoons diced sweet
  pickles
1 cup diced celery
2 tablespoons minced onion

Salt to taste
½ teaspoon pepper
12 slices white bread
Mayonnaise
Lettuce
6 sliced tomatoes

In a medium bowl blend the mayonnaise with the chopped eggs. Add the sweet pickles, celery, onion, salt, and pepper. Toast the bread. Spread a thin layer of the mayonnaise on each slice of bread. Spread 4 slices of bread with the egg mixture. Top with a tomato slice and another slice of bread. Spread a layer of the egg mixture on the second layer. Top with the remaining bread.
Makes 4 sandwiches.

Chipped Beef on Toast

1/4 pound dried beef
2 tablespoons butter
2 10½-ounce cans condensed
  cream of mushroom soup

½ cup light cream
Worcestershire sauce
Salt and pepper to taste
4 slices white bread

Bring a saucepan of water to a boil. Add the dried beef. Cover and boil for 5 minutes. Drain. Cut the beef into thin pieces. Place the beef in the top of a double boiler. Add the butter and cook over direct heat until the butter is melted. Add the mushroom soup and cream and blend until smooth. Season with the Worcestershire sauce, and salt and pepper. Place the pan over boiling water and cook until heated through.
Toast the bread. Spoon the beef mixture over the toast and serve hot.
Makes 6 servings.

*B*arbara McNair co-starred with Elvis in 1970 in *A Change of Habit*. Here she shares memories of her friend.

What were your first impressions when you met Elvis?

"When I first met Elvis, he was so open. He came up to me and said, 'How do you do, Miss McNair? Thank you for working on my film.' He was so gracious, so friendly, so down to earth. We had such a grand time."

What was Elvis like on the set?

"He had a trailer on the set. The trailer was like a house on wheels. It had a big living room with plush couches. He kept a pretty open trailer, and most anybody who was acting in the movie could come on in. He had Cokes and stuff for us, and we'd just sit there and sing until they called us. We'd have such a good time they would have to come and get us out of the trailer and tell us to go back to work."

What kinds of things did Elvis and you talk about?

"When we were inside the trailer, he would be very open with me. He told me that when he was a kid he felt different from other people his age, that he wore sideburns when nobody else was and that he bought his clothes at the navy surplus store. He said he knew he was different from other people and that it had caused him much pain as a young man."

What is one of your fondest memories of him?

"I remember one time when we were watching somebody else film, and the guard came up and said a tour was going to be coming through. They want to see the set. Elvis said, 'Oh, boy, I better run and get all my jewelry and put it on because they'll be expecting me to be wearing my big rings.' And he went and got all decked out. But other than that, he just sat there like everybody else. He was like a big buddy with all of us. He was so gracious. I feel very privileged to have known him." ∎

SIDE DISHES

Asparagus & Ham Casserole

1½ pounds fresh asparagus
½ pound baked ham, sliced
2 tablespoons butter
2 tablespoons all-purpose flour
1 cup milk

½ teaspoon mustard
Salt and pepper to taste
Sugar
1 cup grated American cheese

Clean the asparagus and cut into 1-inch pieces. Boil in lightly salted water. Cook for 15 minutes, until tender. Slice the ham and cut into bite-size cubes. In a double boiler melt the butter and add the flour. Gradually add the milk.

Cook over hot water until the sauce becomes smooth and thick. Add the mustard, salt, and pepper, and a pinch of sugar. Mix in the grated cheese. Cook until the cheese has melted.

Arrange the cooked asparagus and ham on a platter. Pour the sauce over the top. Serve while the sauce is still warm.

Makes 4 servings.

Baked Beans

½ pound sausage
1 21-ounce can baked beans
½ teaspoon mustard

½ cup packed light brown
  sugar
3 tablespoons molasses

In a skillet fry the sausage. Drain on paper towels. Slice into bite-size pieces.

In a medium bowl blend the baked beans with the brown sugar, mustard, and molasses. Add the sausage. Place in a covered casserole dish. Bake at 350° for 15 minutes. Uncover and continue baking for another 15 minutes.

Makes 8 servings.

*O*n May 1, 1957, Elvis went to the MGM studios in Culver City outside Los Angeles to begin recording the soundtrack for his next movie, *Jailhouse Rock*. ■

Bean & Bacon Casserole

6 slices bacon
1 small onion
½ cup ketchup
1 tablespoon mustard
¼ cup molasses
⅓ cup packed light brown
  sugar

1 1-pound can kidney beans
1 1-pound can pork and beans
1 10½-ounce can bean and
  bacon soup

Dice 3 slices of the bacon into small pieces. Dice the onion. In a skillet sauté the bacon with the onion until both are transparent. Add the ketchup, mustard, molasses, and brown sugar. Cook until thoroughly heated and mixture begins to bubble.

In a casserole dish place the kidney beans, pork and beans, and bean and bacon soup. Pour the sautéed onions and bacon on top. Top with the remaining sliced bacon. Bake at 350° for 45 mintues.

Makes 6 servings.

Elvis on the set of Loving You *with Pat Boone.*

*E*lvis's neighbor Pat Boone lived only five minutes away. He
invited Elvis over twice for home-cooked chicken dinners. ■

Butter Beans

4 cups butter beans	⅔ cup light molasses
4 slices bacon	⅔ cup ketchup
½ cup chopped onion	2 tablespoons mustard
1 cup chopped celery	¼ teaspoon salt

Drain the liquid from the beans and reserve ¼ cup. Cut the bacon
into bite-size pieces. In a skillet brown the bacon. Remove the
bacon from the pan. Sauté the onion and celery in the bacon drippings until tender. In a casserole dish combine the beans, bacon,
onion, celery, molasses, ketchup, and mustard. Season with the
salt. Add the reserved liquid from the beans. Bake at 375° for 1
hour and 30 minutes.

Makes 4 servings.

Buttered Green Beans

3 cups green beans
2 tablespoons minced onion
3 tablespoons butter

Salt and pepper to taste
¼ teaspoon paprika

Wash the green beans under cold running water. Pat dry with paper towels. Cut into ½-inch slices.

In a saucepan cook the beans in boiling salted water for 10 minutes or until tender. In a separate saucepan sauté the onions in 1 tablespoon of butter. In a separate pan melt the remaining butter. Drain the green beans.

In a medium bowl toss the green beans with the sautéed onions. Add the remaining melted butter. Season with salt and pepper. Garnish with paprika.

Makes 4 servings.

Green Beans with Bacon

2 8-ounce cans green beans
5 slices bacon
2 tablespoons all-purpose flour
½ cup milk

¾ cup grated Cheddar cheese
2 tablespoons butter
½ cup bread crumbs

Drain the liquid from the green beans and reserve. In a skillet fry the bacon until done. Drain off the fat and blot the bacon with paper towels. Crumble and set aside.

Measure 3 tablespoons of bacon drippings. Blend the drippings with the flour. Stir until smooth. In a saucepan blend the flour mixture with the reserved liquid from the green beans. Add the milk. Stir constantly until the sauce boils and becomes thick and smooth. Add the green beans and cheese. In a small skillet melt the butter and blend in the bread crumbs.

Place the beans in a casserole dish and sprinkle with the breadcrumb mixture. Bake at 325° for 20 minutes. Before serving sprinkle with the crumbled bacon.

Makes 4 servings.

Ham & Green Beans

1 pound fresh green beans
½ cup chopped celery
1 onion, sliced

1½ teaspoons mustard
French dressing
8 slices cooked ham

Slice the beans into quarters. In a soup pot cook the beans in boiling salted water until tender. Drain. In a medium bowl combine the cooked beans with the celery, onion, and mustard. Add French dressing to the desired consistency. Refrigerate for 1 hour. Place the ham on a platter and pour the green beans over the ham.

Makes 4 servings.

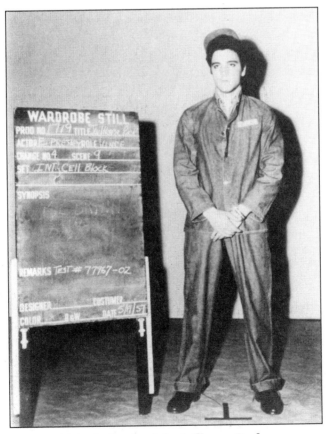

Wardrobe check for Jailhouse Rock.

Succotash

1 thick slice bacon	2 cups lima beans
2 tablespoons minced onion	1 tablespoon butter
½ cup diced celery	½ cup cream
2 cups corn	Salt to taste

In a skillet fry the bacon until crisp. Drain on paper towels. Crumble. Reserve some of the bacon drippings. Sauté the onions and celery in the bacon drippings until tender. Add the corn, lima beans, and bacon. Blend in the butter and cream.

Cook until the vegetables are tender and thoroughly heated. Season with salt to taste.

Makes 4 servings.

*E*lvis always considered himself a big movie fan. "Me and my friends will usually go to the local movie house to watch one and sometimes two movies," he said. "I've seen some movies six times or more, especially those that have something to say." ∎

Fried Cabbage

½ head cabbage	½ teaspoon sugar
2 onions, sliced	2 tablespoons water
¼ cup bacon drippings	2 tablespoons melted butter
¼ teaspoon salt	⅓ cup dry bread crumbs

Cut the cabbage into 6 equal portions. In a skillet sauté the onions in the bacon drippings. Push to one side then add the cabbage. Cook over low heat until the cabbage is browned. Sprinkle one side of the cabbage with the salt and sugar while browing. Turn over and sprinkle again. Add the water and cover. Let simmer for 7 minutes. Turn once during the cooking process. Stir until the onions are mixed well with the cabbage. Sprinkle the butter and bread crumbs over the cabbage.

Makes 4 servings.

Sauerkraut

4 beef bouillon cubes
1½ cups water
1 onion, sliced
⅓ cup bacon drippings

4 cups sauerkraut
1½ teaspoons sugar
2 tablespoons potato

Dissolve the bouillon cubes in the water. Set aside.

In a skillet sauté the onion in the bacon drippings. Add the sauerkraut. Blend in the beef broth and sugar. Simmer over low heat for 1 hour and 30 minutes.

Grate a potato and measure 2 tablespoons. Mix the grated potato into the sauerkraut. Continue to cook for 30 minutes.

Makes 4 servings.

Stuffed Cabbage Rolls

1 head cabbage
1 cup hot water
1 pound ground beef
½ pound ground pork
3 cups cooked rice
1 teaspoon sugar
1 medium chopped onion

½ teaspoon salt
Pepper to taste
1 tablespoon butter
1 10½-ounce can cream
   of tomato soup
½ soup can water

In a large bowl place the cabbage leaves in the hot water. Let the leaves become wilted. In a separate bowl combine the beef, pork, rice, sugar, and onion. Add the salt and pepper.

Place ½ cup of the meat mixture onto each cabbage leaf. Roll up and secure with skewers. Place the rolls in a shallow baking pan. Dot with butter. Combine the soup and water. Pour the mixture over the rolls. Bake at 350° for 1 hour.

Makes 6 servings.

Glazed Carrots with Bacon

3 cups sliced carrots
1 tablespoon packed light
  brown sugar

3 tablespoons melted butter
3 slices bacon
Salt and pepper

In a saucepan drop the carrots into boiling water. Cook until tender. Drain the water and remove the carrots. Add the brown sugar and melted butter to the saucepan. Simmer for 5 minutes.

In a skillet fry the bacon until crisp. Drain on paper towels. Crumble the bacon. Place the cooked carrots in a casserole dish. Pour the sugar/butter syrup over the carrots. Add the bacon. Season with the salt and pepper. Bake at 375° for 20 minutes. Baste the carrots with the syrup during the cooking process.

Makes 4 servings.

Corn Casserole

6 slices bacon
3 tablespoons bacon drippings
6 eggs
½ teaspoon salt

Pepper to taste
1½ cups sweet corn
¼ cup minced onions
1 green bell pepper, sliced

In a skillet fry the bacon to almost crisp. Drain on paper towels. Reserve 3 tablespoons of bacon drippings. Slice the bacon into smaller pieces.

In a medium bowl beat the eggs with the salt and pepper. Add the corn, onions, and bell pepper. Turn into a large skillet with the bacon and drippings. Cook, stirring constantly until the eggs are scrambled. Serve on a warm platter.

Makes 4 servings.

Corn Fritters

2 cups fresh or frozen whole
    corn
½ cup milk
2 cups all-purpose flour

1½ teaspoons salt
3 teaspoons baking powder
2 eggs, well beaten
1 tablespoon butter, melted

Boil the corn in hot salted water until cooked thoroughly. Drain and let the corn cool. In a medium bowl blend the milk and corn. In a separate bowl sift the flour with the salt and baking powder. Add the dry ingredients to the milk and corn mixture. Mix in the eggs and melted butter, and blend thoroughly. Drop by teaspoons into hot oil and fry for 2 minutes or until golden. Remove to waxed paper.

Makes 6 servings.

Taking a break between scenes.

Elvis serenades a very young fan.

Curried Corn Pudding

1 tablespoon butter
¼ cup all-purpose flour
2 cups milk
1 cup cream
4 cups corn

4 egg yolks, beaten
2 teaspoons sugar
1½ teaspoons curry powder
Salt and pepper to taste
4 egg whites, stiffly beaten

Butter a casserole dish and set it aside.

In a saucepan melt the butter. Blend in the flour. Stir until the mixture becomes somewhat thick like a paste. Slowly add the milk. Cook over low heat, stirring constantly, until the mixture comes to a boil and becomes thick. Blend in the cream and simmer, stirring constantly for 5 minutes. Let cool.

Add the corn, egg yolks, sugar, curry powder, salt, and pepper. Blend well. Fold in the egg whites. Spoon into the prepared casserole dish. Place the casserole dish in a larger pan of hot water. Bake at 300° for 1 hour.

Makes 6 servings.

Fried Corn

2 teaspoons bacon drippings
¼ teaspoon salt
3 cups whole corn

1½ cups water
2 tablespoons flour

In a skillet melt the bacon drippings and sprinkle in the salt. Add the corn, water, and flour. Fry the corn over high heat. When it begins to cook, reduce the heat to low.

Let the corn cook slowly until thoroughly done. Spoon the corn into a medium bowl. Scrape the bottom of the skillet and pour the drippings over the corn.

Makes 4 servings.

*W*hile filming *Jailhouse Rock* at MGM, Elvis was given Clark Gable's former dressing room. The studio commissary was more than glad to accommodate his southern tastes by designing a menu for him consisting of crisp bacon, mashed potatoes, and brown gravy. ■

Sautéed Corn with Peppers

1¼ cups chicken stock
2 tablespoons cornstarch
Salt and pepper
¼ cup butter
1 onion, chopped

2 cloves garlic, minced
1 17-ounce can whole-kernel
  corn, drained
2 red bell peppers, diced

In a medium bowl blend the chicken stock with the cornstarch. Season with the salt and pepper. In a skillet melt the butter. Add the onion and garlic, and sauté until the onion is golden. Add the bell peppers and corn. Blend in the chicken stock mixture. Bring to a boil. Stir until the chicken stock begins to thicken slightly. Reduce the heat, cover, and simmer for 2 minutes.

Makes 4 servings.

*O*ne would assume that a night on the town with Elvis would have been truly exciting, but that was not always the case. Because he was so famous, he couldn't risk being seen in public. In Hollywood he usually would take his date to the local drive-in. There they would order sandwiches and plenty of coffee. The evening would be spent talking and driving around for hours looking at all the sights. ■

Fans taking advantage of a photo opportunity with Elvis.

*W*hile Elvis was filming *King Creole*, he lived in the penthouse suite at the Beverly Wilshire. Elvis always ordered plenty of crisp bacon and stacks of white bread for sandwiches from room service and insisted that his friends join him in the lavish, mirrored dining room. There were always gallons of ice-cold Pepsi to drink, and sometimes he would order the house special: the Beverly Wilshire ice cream pie with plenty of extra chocolate sauce. ■

Scalloped Corn

2 tablespoons butter
1 cup bread crumbs
2 eggs

¼ cup milk
Salt and pepper
2 cups whole corn

Butter a casserole dish and set it aside.

In a saucepan melt the butter. Add the bread crumbs and mix thoroughly. In a medium bowl beat the eggs with the milk. Season with the salt and pepper. Place the corn in the prepared casserole dish. Pour the egg mixture over the corn. Blend in the bread crumb mixture. Bake at 325° for 30 minutes.

Makes 4 servings.

Baked Hominy

1 small onion, diced
¼ cup minced green bell pepper
3 tablespoons butter
3 tablespoons all-purpose flour
½ teaspoon dry mustard
Salt and pepper

1½ cups milk
¾ cup grated American cheese
1 24-ounce can whole hominy
¾ cup bread crumbs
3 tablespoons butter

In a skillet sauté the onion and green bell pepper in 3 tablespoons of butter until the onion is golden. Add the flour and dry mustard and season with the salt and pepper. Blend in the milk and cheese. Cook slowly, stirring constantly, until the sauce becomes smooth and somewhat thick.

Drain the hominy. Pour into a casserole dish. Pour the cheese sauce over the hominy and blend well. In a saucepan melt the butter. Blend in the bread crumbs. Pour the crumbs over the top of the casserole. Bake at 375° for 30 minutes.

Makes 4 servings.

Mustard Greens with Bacon

2 pounds fresh mustard greens   4 cups water
½ pound spinach   ½ teaspoon salt
¼ pound sliced bacon   Pepper to taste

Wash the mustard greens and spinach under cold running water. Pat dry with paper towels. In a soup pot place the mustard greens with the bacon and add the water. Cover. Heat to a gentle boil and continue cooking for 45 minutes. Add the salt and season with the pepper. Add the spinach. Cover and cook for 15 minutes more or until the spinach is tender. Water should be added if needed. Serve hot.

Makes 4 servings.

Elvis with Yvonne Lime on the set of Loving You.

Turnip Greens with Bacon

2 pounds fresh turnip greens
4 cups boiling water
¾ teaspoon salt
3 slices bacon
¼ cup chopped onion

1 tablespoon all-purpose flour
¾ teaspoon sugar
½ cup water
1¾ teaspoons vinegar

Wash the turnip greens under cold running water. Drain on paper towels. Place in a soup pot. Add the boiling water and salt. Cover and simmer for 1 hour. Drain.

Cut the bacon into ¼-inch pieces. In a skillet sauté the bacon. Add the onion and continue to sauté for 3 minutes or until the onion is transparent. Add the flour, sugar, ½ cup of water, and vinegar. Simmer for 1 minute or until the mixture becomes thick and smooth. Pour the mixture over the greens. Mix thoroughly. Cook for 5 minutes more.

Makes 4 servings.

Elvis with Mary Ann Mobley
in Harum Scarum.

An afternoon of touch football.

Okra & Tomato Sauté

2 cups okra pods   3 tomatoes, sliced
3 tablespoons bacon drippings   Salt and pepper
2 onions, sliced

Wash the okra pods under cold running water. Pat dry on paper towels. Slice into ¼-inch pieces. Melt the bacon drippings in a skillet. Add the onion and sliced okra. Cover and simmer for 5 minutes or until the onion is tender. Push to one side of the skillet. Add the tomatoes. Cover and continue to simmer until the okra is tender. Toss the tomatoes and okra together. Season with the salt and pepper.
    Makes 4 servings.

*O*ne of Elvis's favorite activities was playing touch football. He would organize games with his boys and other friends. They often played at a little park in Beverly Hills until the crowds got too wild. ■

Pan-Fried Okra

1 pound okra
2 tablespoons butter

Salt and pepper

Wash the okra under running cold water. Cut off the stems and slice. In a skillet melt the butter. Add the okra. Cover and cook for 10 minutes or until the okra is tender. Season with the salt and pepper.
Makes 4 servings.

*B*etween recording sessions, concerts, and films, Elvis spent a lot of time playing touch football. It was one way he could escape from the pressures of his career. He played with old high school buddies and with friends he'd made in Hollywood. Sometimes Elvis would rent an entire football stadium and fill his limousine with Pepsi and sandwiches for everyone. ■

Onion Rings

3 onions
1 tablespoon butter
1¼ cups all-purpose flour
¼ teaspoon salt

Pepper to taste
2 eggs
¾ cup milk
Oil

Slice the onions into ¼-inch rings. Separate the rings and set them aside. In a saucepan melt the butter. Set aside to cool.

In a medium bowl sift together the flour, salt, and pepper. Beat the eggs until fluffy. Add the milk and melted butter. Make a well in the center of the flour mixture. Add the egg mixture. Blend just until smooth.

Dip the onion rings into the batter and coat evenly. Fry in hot oil for 2 minutes or until golden. Remove to paper towels to drain.
Makes 6 servings.

Fried Chick Peas

2 cups dried chick peas	Oil
Water	Salt and pepper to taste

Soak the peas overnight in water.

In a saucepan cook the chick peas in salted water until tender. Drain. In a skillet sauté the peas in hot oil. Season with the salt and pepper.

Makes 4 servings.

*W*hen Elvis returned to Hollywood in 1960 to begin his next film, *G.I. Blues,* he brought an entourage of family and friends. He headed for Los Angeles in a custom-made car that cost $2,424.42 for the two-day trip. As they traveled, Elvis listened to records, ate sandwiches, and drank plenty of Pepsi Cola. When they reached Los Angeles, Elvis was in good spirits and ready to begin working again. ■

Peas in Cream Sauce

½ cup water	1 egg yolk
3 tablespoons butter	¼ cup light cream
2 cups fresh or frozen peas	1 teaspoon sugar
¼ teaspoon salt	

In a saucepan bring the water and butter to a boil. Add the peas and salt. Cover and cook until tender. In a medium bowl beat the egg yolk just to blend. Add the egg yolk to the cream and sugar and beat thoroughly. Add the sauce to the pea mixture. Heat slowly, making sure the peas are tender.

Makes 4 servings.

Baked Potatoes with Salt Pork Gravy

¼ pound salt pork
⅓ cup all-purpose flour
2 cups milk

Salt and pepper to taste
4 potatoes, baked

Cut the salt pork into ¼-inch cubes. In a skillet fry over low heat until brown and crispy. Drain off the fat, reserving ⅓ cup of the drippings. Return the drippings to the skillet and blend with the flour. Add the milk. Cook until the mixture is smooth and thick. Season with the salt and pepper. Pour the gravy inside the baked potatoes. Serve immediately.

Makes 4 servings.

Meeting the press on his return to Hollywood.

Beef & Potato Scallop

2 tablespoons butter
2 tablespoons all-purpose flour
¼ teaspoon salt
Pepper to taste
2 cups milk
1 cup grated Cheddar cheese

4 potatoes
1½ cups dried beef
1 tablespoon minced onion
¼ teaspoon celery salt
Salt and pepper to taste

In a saucepan melt the butter. Blend in the flour. Add the salt and season with pepper. Remove the pan from heat when the sauce begins to boil. Blend in the milk. Stir constantly until the sauce becomes thick and smooth. Let the sauce cool slightly. Blend in ¾ of the grated cheese. Mix until the cheese has melted. Set aside and keep warm.

Wash the potatoes. Peel and cut into bite-size cubes. Mix the potatoes with the dried beef and onion. Add the celery salt. Season with salt and pepper. Blend in with the sauce. Place the potato mixture in a 1-quart casserole dish. Sprinkle the remaining cheese over the top. Bake at 350° for 1 hour or until the potatoes are thoroughly cooked.

Creamed Potatoes

2 tablespoons chopped green
   bell pepper
1 chopped onion
¼ cup butter
2½ tablespoons all-purpose
   flour

2 cups milk
Salt and pepper to taste
3 cups diced potatoes
¾ cup grated Cheddar cheese

In a skillet sauté the onion and green bell pepper in the butter. Blend in the flour. Gradually add the milk. Cook until thick and smooth. Season with the salt and pepper. Add the diced potatoes.

Pour into a casserole dish and top with the grated cheese. Bake at 350° for 30 minutes.

Makes 4 servings.

Elvis with Natalie Wood.

Corned Beef Hash

2 cups chopped cooked corned beef
4 medium potatoes, peeled and diced

2 medium onions, chopped
¼ cup milk
Salt and pepper to taste
2 tablespoons butter

In a mixing bowl toss the corned beef with the potatoes and onions. Add the milk. Season with the salt and pepper.

In a skillet melt the butter. Spread the beef mixture on the bottom of the pan. Flatten. Fry until brown. Turn over and fry the other side. Fold in half and serve on a platter.

Makes 4 servings.

*W*hile still a bachelor in Hollywood, Elvis was linked romantically with Joan Blackman, Tuesday Weld, Ursula Andress, Yvonne Craig, Ann-Margret, Jackie DeShannon, Connie Stevens, Natalie Wood, and Yvonne Lime. ■

French Fries

4 large potatoes	Salt
Oil	

Peel the potatoes. Slice lengthwise into strips ¼-inch thick. Soak in cold water for 1 hour. Drain. Heat oil to 375°. Fry the potatoes until golden brown. Drain and pat dry with paper towels. Season with salt.

Makes 4 servings.

*E*lvis decided to spend an evening with Jana Lund, who appeared with him in *Jailhouse Rock*. Elvis picked Jana up at 7:00 P.M. sharp, and they drove out Wilshire Boulevard toward the ocean. Hours passed as they drove and talked. Finally Elvis decided to head his car back to Hollywood. Passing the Sunset Strip, they headed for the freeway. An hour later they found themselves in Pasadena at a drive-in. Hungry, they ordered one of Elvis's favorite meals, a cheeseburger with Pepsi Cola. ■

Hash Brown Potatoes

4 cups diced potatoes	Salt and pepper
1 chopped onion	¼ cup bacon drippings

In a medium bowl toss together the potatoes and onion. Season with the salt and pepper. In a skillet melt the bacon drippings. Pour in the potatoes. Flatten and sauté over low heat until golden brown. Turn over and sauté the other side until golden. Drain on paper towels before serving.

Makes 4 servings.

Mashed Potatoes & Gravy

4 medium potatoes
2 tablespoons butter
Salt and pepper
Cream
3 tablespoons bacon drippings

3 tablespoons all-purpose flour
½ cup beef stock
1½ cups milk
Salt and pepper

Scrub, peel, and slice the potatoes. Place the potatoes in a pot of boiling salted water. Cook until the potatoes fall apart easily when pierced with a fork. Drain. In a medium bowl mash the potatoes with a fork. Add the butter and blend. Season with the salt and pepper. Pour in the cream to make the potatoes fluffy and light.

In a saucepan melt the bacon drippings. Blend in the flour until smooth and thick. Add the beef stock and milk. Season with the salt and pepper. Add more flour if necessary to thicken. Bring to a boil. Pour over the hot mashed potatoes.

Makes 4 servings.

Elvis on the set of G.I. Blues.

O'Brien Potatoes

2 tablespoons diced green bell
  pepper
2 tablespoons minced onion
3 tablespoons bacon fat

2 tablespoons diced celery
3 cups diced cooked potatoes
3 tablespoons milk
Salt and pepper to taste

In a skillet sauté the green bell peppers and onion in the bacon fat. Add the celery and cook for 5 minutes or until the onion is golden. Add the potatoes and milk. Season with the salt and pepper. Toss thoroughly until well heated. Shape the potato mixture into flattened patties. Brown on the underside.

Makes 6 servings.

On the set of G.I. Blues.

Pan-Fried Potatoes

4 medium potatoes
4 slices bacon

Salt and pepper

Clean, peel, and thinly slice the potatoes. In a saucepan boil the potatoes in salted water. Cook until they fall easily from a fork. Drain. In a skillet fry the bacon until brown. Add the sliced potatoes and continue cooking until the bacon is crisp. Season with the salt and pepper.
Makes 4 servings.

---

*W*hen asked by reporters if he was looking forward to returning to Hollywood after his release from the army, Elvis said, "I was, in a way. I wanted to get out here to make this picture [*G.I. Blues*], but in another way I wouldn't have minded staying at home a little while longer." ■

Potato Pancakes

2 cups grated potatoes
2 eggs, beaten
⅛ teaspoon baking powder
½ teaspoon onion juice

1½ tablespoons all-purpose flour
¾ teaspoon salt

Peel the potatoes and soak them in cold water. Let the potatoes stand in the water overnight.
Drain the water from the potatoes and grate to measure 2 cups. In a medium bowl toss the grated potato with the eggs. Mix while adding the baking powder, onion juice, flour, and salt. Drop from tablespoons into a well-greased skillet. Fry on both sides until golden.
Makes 6 servings.

Elvis on the set of Loving You.

*A*fter a busy day at the studio, Elvis liked to unwind with his friends back at his suite at the Beverly Wilshire. Elvis arranged ahead of time for plenty of sandwiches and Pepsi to be waiting for them when they arrived. ■

Spiced Potatoes

4 slices bacon	½ teaspoon diced celery
4 cups raw potato	1 teaspoon sugar
1 onion, sliced	½ teaspoon mustard
2 cups stewed tomatoes	Salt and pepper to taste

In a skillet fry the bacon until done. Drain on paper towels. Crumble and set aside.

Peel and slice the potatoes to measure 4 cups. Place the potatoes and onion into the bacon drippings. Sauté for 8 minutes, stirring constantly. Add the tomatoes, celery, sugar, and mustard. Season with the salt and pepper. Simmer for 20 minutes or until the potatoes are tender. Before serving crumble bacon over the top.

Makes 4 servings.

To the movie industry, releasing an Elvis Presley movie was like money in the bank. ■

Creole Rice

1 medium onion, chopped	Salt and pepper to taste
1 thick slice cooked ham, chopped	Paprika
	Bread crumbs
2 cups stewed tomatoes	1 cup boiled white rice
1 tablespoon butter	

In a medium bowl combine the onion, ham, tomatoes, and butter. Season with the salt, pepper, and paprika. Blend thoroughly. Add the white rice. Place in a covered casserole dish. Sprinkle the bread crumbs on top. Bake at 400° for 15 mintues.

Makes 4 servings.

Visiting with members of the royal families of Sweden,
Norway, and Denmark on the set of G.I. Blues.

Candied Sweet Potatoes

6 medium sweet potatoes   ⅓ cup packed light brown sugar
⅓ cup butter   Salt to taste

Wash the sweet potatoes. In a saucepan boil the potatoes in water to cover for 35 minutes, until tender. Drain. Dry potatoes over very low heat while shaking the pan. Peel and set aside.

In a skillet melt the butter over low heat. Blend in the brown sugar, and season with the salt. Cook until the mixture begins to boil. Add the potatoes. Continue cooking over medium heat for 20 minutes or until the potatoes are well coated. Turn the potatoes several times during the cooking process.

Makes 4 servings.

*O*nce when Elvis's black Lincoln Continental pulled up in front of The Cloister, a famous nightclub on Hollywood's Sunset Strip, his boys stepped out first and then Elvis. Fans swarmed the car, and it was nearly ten minutes before Juliet Prowse, his date for the evening, was able to emerge from it. ■

Ham & Sweet Potatoes

1½ pounds cooked ham	2 tablespoons packed brown
1 16-ounce can sweet potatoes	sugar

Slice the ham and place it under the broiler for 5 minutes. Turn the ham over. Place the sweet potatoes around the ham. Sprinkle the brown sugar over the top of mixture. Broil 5 minutes more or until lightly browned.

Makes 4 servings.

Meeting princesses from Sweden, Norway, and Denmark on the set of G.I. Blues.

*E*lvis Presley was a home-town boy from Memphis who enjoyed the simple life: good home-cooked meals, fancy cars, and making millions. ■

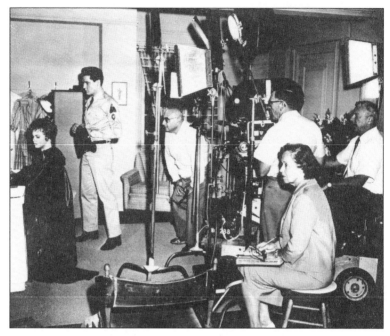

On the set of G. I. Blues *with Juliet Prowse.*

Scalloped Green Tomatoes

2 medium green tomatoes, sliced   2 tablespoons sugar
1 chopped onion   1 tablespoon butter
1 ripe tomato, chopped   1 cup dried bread crumbs
Salt and pepper   ½ cup evaporated milk

Butter a casserole dish and set it aside.

Place the green tomatoes in a saucepan with the onion, ripe tomato, salt, pepper, and sugar. Cover and cook for 5 minutes over low heat, shaking pan frequently. In a saucepan melt the butter and blend in ½ cup of bread crumbs.

Place the other ½ cup of the bread crumbs in the bottom of the prepared casserole dish. Spoon the tomato mixture over the crumbs. Pour the evaporated milk over the tomatoes. Spread the remaining butter/bread-crumb mixture over the top. Bake at 400° for 10 to 15 minutes or until brown.

Makes 4 servings.

Corn & Zucchini

6 small zucchini
1 green bell pepper, diced
1 medium onion, diced
3 tablespoons butter
1 16-ounce can tomatoes, drained

1 8-ounce can whole kernel
  corn, drained
Salt and pepper
⅓ cup grated Parmesan cheese

Wash the zucchini. Peel and cut into ⅛-inch slices. In a saucepan sauté the onion and green bell pepper in the butter until golden. Add the zucchini. Simmer for 10 minutes or until tender. Add the tomatoes and corn to the zucchini. Season with the salt and pepper. Heat thoroughly.

Place the corn and zucchini mixture in a casserole dish. Sprinkle the Parmesan cheese over the top. Broil for 2 minutes until the cheese is brown.

Makes 4 servings.

Mixed Vegetables

1 pound carrots
1 pound fresh peas
¼ cup sliced green beans
¼ cup whole corn
½ teaspoon sugar
1 cup boiling water

¼ teaspoon salt
2 tablespoons all-purpose flour
2 tablespoons butter, melted
Salt and pepper to taste
¾ cup buttermilk
¼ cup mayonnaise

Clean and peel the carrots. Slice into ½-inch pieces. In a soup pot add the carrots, peas, green beans, corn, and sugar to rapidly boiling water. Add the salt. Cover and cook for 10 minutes or until the vegetables are tender. Drain.

In the top of a double boiler blend the flour and butter. Season with the salt and pepper. Add the buttermilk and stir constantly until the sauce is thick and smooth. Blend in the mayonnaise. Continue cooking until the sauce is thoroughly heated. Pour over the hot vegetables.

Makes 4 servings.

*S*heree North co-starred with Elvis in *The Trouble with Girls* in 1969. Here she tells about working with Elvis.

When did you first meet Elvis?

"On the first day I came to the set, there was a huge bouquet in my dressing room with a note from Elvis. That was so sweet. Of course, I went right out to meet him and thank him. He was just great. He was terrific to just sit around and talk to."

What is one of your fondest memories of working with Elvis?

"One time my mom wanted to see Elvis. She just loved Elvis and had made him a bag of cookies. Elvis and I were sitting around laughing, talking, joking. When my mom came on the set, he jumped out of his seat. At first I thought he was kidding. He got very serious and very respectful and called her ma'am. I kept saying, 'Elvis, it's my mom,' but he wouldn't sit down. He would only stand in her presence. I said, 'Sit down, Elvis. It's my mom.' He took the cookies and thanked her.

I said, 'Mom, he doesn't want to eat those cookies,' but he said, 'No ma'am, these are wonderful cookies.' And he ate one in front of her. I thought, who is this guy? He was just so respectful. All those things you think guys should be with your mother—Elvis actually was."

What are some of the things you talked about?

"Elvis had a soulful quality. He talked about the time when he heard about his mom's death and how he felt he couldn't cry in front of the others. So at night when everybody else was more or less asleep, he would put the pillows over his head and really cry. He felt he couldn't show any weakness. He talked about how people didn't understand that even if you were a star, you have pain."

What was he like to work with?

"He liked it if you treated him like a normal person and not Elvis, larger than life. We had some guys on the set who did some songs in the show, and Elvis made an effort to kid around with them. He was just one of the guys. The time I spent with him will always be with me." ■

DESSERTS

Almond Pound Cake

1 cup cake flour	¼ cup almond paste
¼ teaspoon salt	2 tablespoons milk
3 egg yolks	½ teaspoon vanilla extract
2 eggs	⅓ cup melted butter
1 cup sugar	

Grease an 11 x 7-inch baking pan and set it aside.

In a medium bowl sift the flour. Remeasure 1 cup of flour. Sift again with the salt. In a separate bowl combine the egg yolks and eggs. Place the bowl in a pan of hot water. Continue beating the eggs until thoroughly blended. Gradually add the sugar while beating.

Combine the almond paste and the milk. Add the vanilla and a little of the egg yolk mixture. Blend until smooth. Pour back into the egg mixture. Blend in the flour mixture. Add the melted butter. Pour the batter into the prepared pan. Bake at 350° for 30 minutes. Invert the cake onto a cloth-covered cooling rack. To serve, cut into squares and top with whipping cream.

Makes 8 servings.

Elvis with members of the crew on the set of Follow That Dream.

Banana Split Cake

1¼ cups all-purpose flour	¼ cup milk
1 cup sugar	2 eggs
1 teaspoon baking soda	1 cup mashed ripe bananas
½ teaspoon salt	3 ripe bananas, peeled and sliced
½ cup softened butter	1½ cups whipped cream

Grease and flour a 9 x 9-inch cake pan and set it aside.

In a large mixing bowl combine the flour, sugar, baking soda, salt, butter, milk, eggs, and mashed bananas. Beat with an electric mixer just until the dry ingredients are moist. Scrape the batter from the sides of the bowl and increase the speed, beating for 3 minutes more. Pour the batter into the prepared pan. Bake at 350° for 40 minutes. Let cool.

To serve, cut into squares. Split each piece in half lengthwise. Layer the bottom portion with the sliced bananas and whipped cream. Replace the upper portion of the cake.

Makes 6 servings.

Brown Sugar Cake

2 cups all-purpose flour
2 cups packed dark brown sugar
½ cup butter

1 egg
1 cup sour milk
½ teaspoon baking soda

Grease and flour two 9-inch cake pans and set them aside.

In a large bowl combine the flour, sugar, and butter. Remove 1 cup of the mixture and set aside.

In a separate bowl beat the egg with the milk. Add the baking soda. Combine with the flour mixture. Pour into the prepared pans. Sprinkle the reserved flour mixture on top. Bake at 350° for 35 minutes.

Makes 8 servings.

Buttermilk Cake

⅓ cup butter
1 cup sugar
2 eggs
1½ cups all-purpose flour
1 teaspoon baking soda
2 teaspoons baking powder
¼ teaspoon salt
1 teaspoon vanilla extract
1 cup buttermilk

½ teaspoon ground cloves
1 teaspoon ground cinnamon
½ teaspoon ground allspice
3 tablespoons melted butter
3 tablespoons cream
5 tablespoons packed light
  brown sugar
½ cup chopped walnuts

In a medium bowl cream the butter with the sugar. Separate the eggs. Set aside the egg whites. Beat the egg yolks and add to the creamed butter. In a separate bowl sift the flour, baking soda, baking powder, and salt. Add the dry ingredients to the batter with the vanilla. Beat the egg whites until stiff. Fold the egg whites into the batter. Bake at 350° for 35 minutes. Let cool.

In a saucepan melt the butter. Add the cream, brown sugar, and nuts. Boil for 5 minutes. Spread the topping over the cake.

Makes 6 servings.

Lemon Coconut Cake

½ cup butter
1 cup sugar
1¾ cups cake flour
1¾ teaspoons baking powder
¼ teaspoon salt
½ cup milk
1 teaspoon grated lemon rind
½ cup grated coconut
3 egg whites
⅔ cup sugar
3½ tablespoons cornstarch
⅛ teaspoon salt
¾ cup water

1 egg
1 tablespoon butter
1½ teaspoons grated lemon rind
¼ cup lemon juice
2 cups sugar
⅔ cup water
2 tablespoons corn syrup
2 egg whites
⅛ teaspoon salt
1½ teaspoons vanilla extract
1½ cups grated coconut

Flour two 9-inch layer cake pans. Line with waxed paper. Set aside.

Cream the butter until soft. Add ½ cup of the sugar and beat until fluffy. Sift the cake flour with the baking powder and ¼ teaspoon of salt. Add the dry ingredients to the creamed butter with the milk. Mix until smooth. Add the lemon rind and coconut. Beat 3 egg whites until foamy. Add ½ cup of sugar and beat until peaks form. Fold into the batter. Pour the batter into the prepared pans. Bake at 375° for 20 minutes. Let the layers cool somewhat. Turn onto a cooling rack. Remove the waxed paper and cool.

For the filling, blend ⅔ cup of sugar, cornstarch, flour, and ⅛ teaspoon of salt in the top of a double boiler. Add the water. Cook over boiling water until thickened. Cover and continue cooking for 10 minutes. Beat the egg. Blend some of the hot mixture into the egg. Return to the double boiler. Reduce the heat and cook 2 minutes more. Stir so the filling won't burn. Remove the pan from the heat. Add the butter and lemon rind. Chill. Add the lemon juice.

For the frosting, blend 2 cups of sugar with the water and corn syrup in a saucepan. Stir over low heat until the sugar is dissolved. Cover and boil for 2 minutes. Uncover and continue to boil until the mixture reaches a soft ball stage. Remove the pan from the heat. Beat 2 egg whites with ⅛ teaspoon of salt until stiff. Pour the mixture into the egg whites. Add the vanilla. Beat until the frosting thickens. Add the coconut.

Spread the filling over 1 layer of cake. Top with the other layer. Spread the frosting over the top and sides of the cake.

Makes 8 servings.

Elvis greeting fans on the set of Flaming Star.

Chocolate Chip Chiffon Cake

1 cup plus 2 tablespoons cake
   flour
¾ cup plus 2 tablespoons sugar
1½ teaspoons baking powder
½ teaspoon salt
¼ cup cooking oil
3 egg yolks

⅓ cup water
1 teaspoon almond extract
5 egg whites
¼ teaspoon cream of tartar
1½ ounces semisweet
   chocolate, grated

In a medium bowl sift the cake flour. Remeasure 1 cup plus 2 tablespoons of cake flour. Resift with ½ cup of the sugar, baking powder,
and salt. Make a well in the center. Add the cooking oil, egg yolks,
water, and almond extract. Beat until smooth. Set the bowl aside.

In a separate bowl beat the egg whites until frothy. Add cream of
tartar. Beat well until the egg whites form stiff peaks. Gradually add
the remaining sugar. Slowly pour the egg yolk mixture over the surface of the egg white mixture. Fold until completely blended.
Sprinkle the grated chocolate over the top.

Pour into a 9 x 9-inch baking pan. Bake at 350° for 35 minutes or
until cake tests done. Invert the pan between the edges of two other
pans. Let the cake cool, making sure that the cake is not touching
any surface.

Makes 6 servings.

Chocolate Cake

2½ cups cake flour
⅓ cup cocoa
¾ teaspoons baking soda
1½ teaspoons baking powder
1 teaspoon salt
⅔ cup butter
1¾ cups sugar
2 eggs
1½ cups ice water

½ teaspoon vanilla extract
½ cup butter
2½ squares unsweetened
  chocolate
3 cups confectioners' sugar
¼ teaspoon salt
1 egg
1 teaspoon vanilla
4-ounce chocolate bar, grated

Grease two 9-inch cake pans and set them aside.

In a medium bowl sift the flour, cocoa, baking soda, baking powder, and salt. In a separate bowl cream the butter with the sugar. Blend until smooth. Add the eggs, one at a time. Beat until smooth and fluffy. Add the flour mixture and water alternately. Add the vanilla. Pour the batter into the prepared pans. Bake at 350° for 25 minutes or until cake tests done. Cool on a cake rack.

In a saucepan melt the butter and unsweetened chocolate over low heat. Add the confectioners' sugar and salt. Blend until smooth. Pour the chocolate mixture into a medium bowl. Place the bowl in a pan of ice water. Beat until the frosting thickens.

Refrigerate for 20 minutes. Immediately frost the tops and sides of both cakes. Place one cake on top of the other. Garnish with grated chocolate bar.

Makes 8 servings.

Chocolate Spice Cake

3 ounces unsweetened chocolate
2¾ cups cake flour
4 teaspoons baking powder
½ teaspoon salt
1 teaspoon ground cloves
1 teaspoon ground allspice
1 teaspoon ground cinnamon
1 cup butter
1½ cups sugar

4 eggs, beaten
1¼ cups milk
3 ounces unsweetened
  chocolate
½ teaspoon vanilla extract
¼ cup cream
⅓ cup cream cheese
2½ cups sifted confectioners'
  sugar

Grease a 9-inch tube pan and set it aside.

In a saucepan melt 3 ounces of chocolate. Let it cool thoroughly. In a medium bowl sift the flour. Remeasure 2¾ cups of cake flour. Sift again with the baking powder, salt, cloves, allspice, and cinnamon. In a large bowl cream the butter with the sugar until light and fluffy. Add the beaten eggs and cooled chocolate. Beat until smooth. Add the flour mixture to the chocolate mixture with the milk. Blend thoroughly. Pour into the prepared pan. Bake at 350° for 1 hour.

In a saucepan melt 3 ounces of chocolate. Add the vanilla and cream. In a medium bowl soften the cream cheese in the melted chocolate. Add the desired amount of the confectioners' sugar for an even spreading consistency. Beat until smooth and creamy. Frost the tops and sides of cooled cake.

Makes 8 servings.

*T*he basic ingredients to an Elvis get-together consisted of easy conversation and a good stock of food, including peanut butter and chocolate milk. For entertainment there was music and television. ■

Elvis signing autographs on the set
of Follow That Dream.

Maraschino Cherry Cake

2½ cups cake flour
3¾ teaspoons baking soda
Salt
½ cup butter
1 cup sugar
2 eggs
⅔ cup milk
⅓ cup cherry juice

1 egg white
⅛ teaspoon cream of tartar
Salt to taste
3 tablespoons cold water
¾ cup sugar
½ teaspoon vanilla extract
1½ teaspoons light corn syrup
½ cup sliced cherries

Grease two 8-inch cake pans. Line the bottoms with waxed paper. Grease the waxed paper. Set the pans aside.

In a medium bowl sift the cake flour. Remeasure 2½ cups of flour and resift 3 times with the baking powder and salt. In a separate bowl cream the butter with the sugar. Add the eggs, one at a time. Beat until smooth and fluffy. Add the flour mixture, the milk, and cherry juice alternately. Fold in the sliced cherries. Pour the batter into the prepared pans. Bake at 350° for 30 minutes. Turn out on a cake rack. Remove the waxed paper to finish cooling.

In the top of a double boiler over simmering water combine the egg white, cream of tartar, salt, cold water, and sugar. The pan should not touch the water. Beat for 8 minutes or until the mixture forms peaks. Remove the pan from the heat. Change the water in the bottom of the double boiler from hot to cold and replace the pan. Add the vanilla and corn syrup. Continue beating until the frosting is thick and smooth. Immediately frost the tops and sides of both cakes. Place one cake on top of the other.

Makes 6 servings.

*N*orman Taurog, who directed Elvis in five of his movies, told of the day Elvis arrived at his Beverly Hills home and asked him to come outside and look at his new Cadillac. Elvis asked the director if he liked the car. "Yes," the director responded. As Elvis said good-bye to Taurog, they shook hands. Inside Elvis's palm were the keys to the new car. He placed them into Taurog's and said, "Enjoy." ■

Elvis on location in Florida for Follow That Dream.

Orange Chiffon Cake

1 cup all-purpose flour
¾ cup sugar
1½ teaspoons baking powder
¼ teaspoon salt
¼ cup oil
3 egg yolks
2 tablespoons water
¼ cup orange juice

3 tablespoons grated orange
rind
4 egg whites
¼ teaspoon cream of tartar
3 cups confectioners' sugar
⅓ cup butter
3 tablespoons orange juice
Grated orange rind

In a medium bowl sift together the flour, sugar, baking powder, and salt. Make a well in the center of the ingredients. Pour in the oil, egg yolks, water, orange juice, and orange rind. Mix thoroughly until well blended and smooth. In a separate bowl whip the egg whites until stiff peaks begin to form. Add the cream of tartar. Pour the egg yolk mixture over the egg whites. Fold until well blended. Pour the batter into an ungreased 8-inch cake pan. Bake at 350° for 30 minutes or until a toothpick inserted in the center comes out clean. Invert and let cool.

In a small bowl blend together the confectioners' sugar and butter. Beat until smooth and creamy. Add the orange juice and blend well. After the cake has cooled frost with the frosting. Garnish with grated orange rind.

Makes 6 servings.

Peach Upside-Down Cake

Sugar
Cinnamon
Sliced fresh peaches
¾ cup all-purpose flour
½ cup sugar
1 teaspoon baking powder

⅛ teaspoon baking soda
⅛ teaspoon salt
1 egg
½ cup sour cream
Whipped cream

Grease the bottom and sides of a 9-inch baking dish with butter. Sprinkle equal amounts of the sugar and cinnamon inside. Cover with a layer of the peaches. Sprinkle on top of the peaches more of the sugar. Cover and bake at 300° for 10 minutes.

In a medium bowl sift together the flour, sugar, baking powder, baking soda, and salt. In a separate bowl beat the egg into the sour cream. Add to the flour mixture. Beat until smooth. Pour the batter over the baked peaches. Bake at 350° for 20 minutes or until a toothpick inserted in the center comes out clean. To serve invert on a plate. Top with whipped cream.

Makes 6 servings.

Elvis getting in shape for Kid Galahad.

*E*lvis won three Grammy awards from the National Academy of Recording Arts and Sciences, all in the gospel category. In 1967 he won the best sacred performance award for "How Great Thou Art." In 1972 he won the best inspirational performance award for "He Touched Me." In 1974 he won the best inspirational performance award for "How Great Thou Art." ■

Peanut Butter Cake

2 cups plus 2 tablespoons cake
   flour
¾ teaspoon baking soda
1¼ teaspoons baking powder
¼ teaspoon salt
¼ cup butter
⅓ cup peanut butter
1⅓ cups sugar
2 eggs

⅔ cup buttermilk
⅓ cup fresh orange juice
16 ounces semisweet chocolate
½ cup butter
3 cups confectioners' sugar
¼ teaspoon salt
1 teaspoons ground cinnamon
1 cup milk, warmed
2 teaspoons vanilla extract

Grease two 9-inch cake pans. Line the bottoms with waxed paper. Grease the waxed paper. Set the pans aside.

In a medium bowl sift the flour. Remeasure 2 cups plus 2 tablespoons of flour. Resift 5 times with the baking soda, baking powder, and salt. In a large bowl cream the butter and peanut butter until smooth. Add the sugar and eggs, one at a time. Beat until smooth and fluffy. Add the flour mixture. Blend the buttermilk with the orange juice and add it to the batter a little at a time. Blend until smooth. Pour the batter into the prepared pans. Bake at 350° for 30 minutes or until a toothpick inserted in the center comes out clean. Let the cake cool for 10 minutes. Turn out on a cake rack. Remove the waxed paper to finish cooling.

In the top of a double boiler over simmering water melt the chocolate. Add the butter and stir until smooth. Blend in the confectioners' sugar, salt, and cinnamon. Add the milk and vanilla, and blend until smooth. Let cool. Frost the tops and sides of both cakes. Place one cake on top of the other.

Makes 6 servings.

Pineapple Upside-Down Cake

1½ cups cake flour
2½ teaspoons baking powder
¼ teaspoon salt
⅓ cup butter
⅔ cup sugar
1 egg
¾ teaspoon vanilla extract

½ cup milk
3 tablespoons butter
3 tablespoons packed light
   brown sugar
1 14-ounce can pineapple rings
Maraschino cherries
Whipped Cream

Grease an 8 x 8-inch baking pan and set it aside.

In a medium bowl sift the flour. Remeasure 1½ cups of flour. Sift again with the baking powder and salt. In a separate bowl cream the butter with the sugar. Blend until light and fluffy. Add the beaten egg and vanilla. Beat thoroughly. Add the flour mixture alternately with the milk to the butter mixture.

In a saucepan melt the 3 tablespoons of butter. Coat the bottom of the prepared pan with the melted butter. Sprinkle the brown sugar over the butter. Arrange the pineapple rings in the pan. Place the cherries in the centers of the pineapple rings.

Pour the batter over the pineapple rings. Bake at 350° for 45 minutes. Invert the pan onto a cooling pan. Let cool for 1 minute before removing. Serve with the whipped cream.

Makes 6 servings.

*B*ye, *Bye, Birdie* is loosely based on Elvis's own experiences of an up-and-coming rock 'n' roll star being drafted into the army. ∎

Sour Cream Cake

2 cups cake flour	2 eggs
1½ teaspoons baking powder	1 cup sugar
¼ teaspoon salt	1 cup sour cream
½ teaspoon baking soda	1 teaspoon vanilla extract

Grease an 8 x 8-inch baking pan. Line the pan with waxed paper. Set it aside.

In a medium bowl sift the cake flour. Remeasure 2 cups of flour. Sift again with the baking powder, salt, and baking soda. In a large bowl beat the eggs until thick. Add the sugar. Mix thoroughly. Add the flour mixture to the egg mixture with the sour cream and vanilla. Pour the batter into the prepared pan. Bake at 350° for 35 minutes.

Makes 4 servings.

*E*lvis and Yvonne Lime dated briefly when he was working in Hollywood. He laughed and asked, "When are we going to get together?"

"How about the end of the week?" she said. "Let's have a picnic. I'll bring my friends from Glendale. You bring your boys from Memphis."

When the caravan convened on Friday evening, forty-four kids were all set to go to the beach. Part of Yvonne's group went ahead to set up the food, and the rest followed one hour later. They arrived at the beach as planned, but a freak storm came up—almost a cloudburst. Everyone ran for the cars, with Elvis shouting, "Keep driving north, we'll escape the storm." Elvis apparently thought the storm was headed south, and so they drove for an hour, an hour of hysterical laughs. But instead of driving out of the storm, they drove into it!

Finally, at Trancas Beach they stopped and Elvis said, "Let's go back to the hotel. We'll have a picnic in my suite."

So they all headed back, although one car—the one with the food—didn't get the message. Elvis and his friends got back. When Yvonne, who was wearing pedal pushers, arrived, she tried to get past the lobby and into the elevator to Elvis's suite but was stopped.

"They thought I was trying to crash his place," she laughed. "I told them what had happened, but you can imagine how silly that sounded. So I said to myself, OK, I'll just go down to the corner and call him from there, and then you'll see. I didn't realize I'd still have to go through their switchboard, but it worked. They called Elvis, and he laughed himself sick. He said it was OK for me to come up, of course."

"The gang was starved, but there was no food. So Elvis sent out for hamburgers, baked beans, and so forth. It was more fun than we could have cooked up on the beach. It sure was a lot more hectic, too.

Then someone suggested that Elvis sing. But there was no guitar in the suite. Elvis had left his at the studio! "Let's go buy one," he said. But where? It was now almost 9:00 P.M. Someone remembered Music City on Vine Street.

So the kids all piled back into their cars and caravaned down to the store. Imagine the clerk's surprise when she looked up and there was Elvis Presley smiling at her and saying, "I'd like to buy a guitar."

The musical instrument department was closed, so everyone returned to the hotel suite where they laughed it up, singing and fooling around until early in the morning. ∎

Apple Chiffon Pie

1 packet unflavored gelatin	1 teaspoon grated lemon rind
¼ cup water	2 tablespoons fresh lemon juice
3 eggs, separated	1½ cups chunky applesauce
½ cup molasses	1 9-inch baked pie shell
¼ teaspoon salt	

In a small bowl blend the gelatin in the water. In a medium bowl beat the egg yolks just until blended. Do not overbeat. Add the molasses, salt, lemon rind, and lemon juice. Mix thoroughly. Place in the top portion of a double boiler. Cook over boiling water, stirring constantly, until thick and smooth. Remove and add the gelatin. Stir to dissolve. Add the chunky applesauce. Refrigerate until well chilled.

Beat the egg whites until stiff peaks appear. Blend the apple mixture into the egg whites. Pour the filling into the pie shell. Return the pie to the refrigerator. Chill until filling is firm.

Makes 6 servings.

Elvis and Yvonne Lime

Boston Cream Pie

2 cups sifted cake flour
2 teaspoons baking powder
¼ teaspoon salt
½ cup butter
1 cup sifted sugar
6 egg yolks, divided
2 teaspoons vanilla extract, divided

2¼ cups milk, divided
1 vanilla bean
½ cup sugar
¼ cup all-purpose flour
2 cups confectioners' sugar
2 tablespoons hot milk
2 tablespoons cocoa

Grease two 8-inch round cake pans and set them aside.

In a medium bowl resift the flour with the baking powder and salt. In a separate bowl cream the butter. Gradually add the sifted sugar, creaming until light. Beat in 3 egg yolks. Blend in 1 teaspoon of vanilla. Add the dry ingredients alternately with ¾ cup of milk. Stir until smooth after each addition. Pour the batter into the prepared pans. Bake at 375° for 25 minutes.

In a saucepan scald the remaining 1½ cups of milk with the vanilla bean. In the top of a double boiler over simmering water mix ½ cup of sugar, the flour, and the remaining 3 egg yolks. Beat the mixture until light. Remove the vanilla bean from the milk and gradually pour the milk into the egg mixture. Stir until well blended. Cook, stirring constantly, until the filling begins to thicken. Remove the pan from the water and stir until the mixture begins to cool. Set the filling aside to cool completely.

In a medium bowl blend the confectioners' sugar into the hot milk. Add the remaining 1 teaspoon of vanilla and the cocoa, and blend until smooth.

Spread the filling over one layer of the cake. Top with the remaining layer. Frost the cake with the frosting.

Makes 6 servings.

Apple Crisp

4 cups cooking apples
1 tablespoon fresh lemon juice
1 cups oats
½ teaspoon salt
1 teaspoon ground cinnamon

½ cup packed light brown
  sugar
⅓ cup all-purpose flour, sifted
⅓ cup melted butter

Grease a shallow 9 x 13-inch casserole dish and set it aside.

Peel, core, and slice the apples. Place them in the prepared casserole dish. Sprinkle with the lemon juice. In a medium bowl combine the oats, salt, cinnamon, brown sugar, and flour. Toss thoroughly. Add the melted butter. Mix until the dough becomes crumbly. Pour the topping over the apples. Bake at 375° for 30 minutes.

*I*f Elvis wanted to impress his date for an evening, he would order an intimate dinner to be served in the penthouse suite of the hotel. Afterward they would watch television or listen to records. ■

Apple Pie

Pastry for 1 9-inch double
  crust pie
1 cup sugar
2 tablespoons all-purpose flour
1 teaspoon ground cinnamon

¼ teaspoon salt
5 cups peeled and chopped
  apples
1 tablespoon fresh lemon juice
2 tablespoons butter, melted

Line a pie tin with half of the pastry and set it aside.

In a medium bowl combine the sugar, flour, cinnamon, and salt. Sprinkle half the mixture into the pie shell. Cover with the apples. Sprinkle the remaining mixture over the apples. Top with the lemon juice. Dot with the melted butter. Cover the pie with the remaining dough. Pinch to seal the dough. Bake at 425° for 35 minutes or until the crust is golden brown.

Makes 6 servings.

Chocolate Walnut Pie

3 tablespoons butter	½ cup chopped walnuts
¼ cup packed light brown sugar	½ teaspoon vanilla extract
	⅛ teaspoon salt
½ cup corn syrup	½ cup raisins
1 egg, beaten	1 cup chocolate chips
2 teaspoons vinegar	1 9-inch unbaked pie shell

In a medium bowl cream together the butter and brown sugar. Beat until fluffy. Add the corn syrup and egg. Blend in the vinegar, walnuts, vanilla, salt, and raisins. Place the chocolate chips in the bottom of the pie shell. Pour the filling over the chips. Bake at 425° for 5 minutes. Reduce the heat to 350° and bake for 15 minutes more. Let cool slightly.

Makes 6 servings.

"*T*he fans send me lots of presents, mostly cakes and cookies."—Elvis ∎

Coconut Cream Pie

1 cup coconut milk	2 eggs, separated
1 cup milk	1½ cups fresh shredded coconut
⅔ cup sugar	
¼ teaspoon salt	1 tablespoon butter
2 tablespoons cornstarch	½ teaspoon vanilla extract
3 tablespoons all-purpose flour	1 9-inch baked pie shell

In the top of a double boiler over direct heat, bring the coconut milk and ½ cup of milk just to boiling. In a medium bowl add all but ¼ cup of the sugar to the salt, cornstarch, flour, and the remaining milk. Blend until the batter develops into a smooth paste. Add the paste to the milk in the double boiler. Cook over direct heat until the mixture boils and becomes thick. Place the pan over boiling water and continue cooking for 5 minutes more, stirring frequently. In a separate bowl beat the egg yolks. Add a few spoonfuls of the hot mixture to the eggs. Continue beating and return the eggs to the double boiler. Stir well to blend.

Remove the pan from the heat and add 1 cup of coconut, the butter, and vanilla. Pour the filling into the pie shell. In a separate bowl beat the egg whites until foamy. Add ¼ cup of sugar a little at a time. Beat until smooth and stiff. Spread on top of the pie filling. Sprinkle the remaining coconut over the top. Bake at 350° for 12 minutes. Cool thoroughly before serving.

Makes 6 servings.

Elvis, That's the Way It Is.

"Las Vegas—The MGM crew, headed by director Dennis Sanders, here to film Elvis Presley's appearance at the International Hotel, reports that as a result of his appearance: nine couples have named their children Elvis; four young men are making every attempt to look like the star; five fans over 80 will attend every show through Labor Day; 31 fans will attend both shows a night; three camper vans are covered with pictures of Elvis; and fans from 32 states and 16 countries are gathered here just for the event."—*The Hollywood Reporter,* August 17, 1970 ■

Ice Cream Pie

5 squares unsweetened chocolate
¾ cup sugar
2 cups boiling water
¼ cup light corn syrup
½ teaspoon salt
1¼ cups graham cracker
  crumbs

⅓ cup butter, melted
¼ cup sugar
½ teaspoon ground cinnamon
1 quart vanilla ice cream,
  softened
1 chocolate bar, grated

In a saucepan melt the 5 squares of chocolate. Cook over low heat for 3 minutes, stirring constantly, until smooth. Add ¾ cup of sugar, corn syrup, and salt. Continue cooking for 4 minutes. Let the mixture cool.

In a medium bowl combine the graham cracker crumbs, melted butter, ¼ cup of sugar, and cinnamon. Evenly press the mixture into the bottom of a 9-inch pie tin. Refrigerate until the crust becomes firm.

Fill the crust with the ice cream. Top with the chocolate syrup. Garnish with the grated chocolate. Refrigerate until the ice cream is set.

Makes 6 servings.

*Taking a break on the set
of* Kissin' Cousins.

Strawberry Chiffon Pie

1¼ cups graham cracker
  crumbs
⅓ cup butter
¼ cup sugar
½ teaspoon ground cinnamon
1 pint strawberries, washed and
  dried
¾ cup sugar
1 packet unflavored gelatin

¼ cup cold water
½ cup hot water
1 tablespoon fresh lemon juice
Salt
½ cup heavy cream
2 egg whites
Strawberries, sliced
Cream

In a medium bowl combine the graham cracker crumbs, melted butter, sugar, and cinnamon. Evenly press the mixture into the bottom of a 9-inch pie tin. Refrigerate until the crust becomes firm.

In a medium bowl crush the strawberries. Coat with ½ cup of the sugar. Set aside for 20 minutes. In a separate bowl add the gelatin to ¼ cup of cold water. Add ½ cup of hot water to dissolve. Add the gelatin mixture to the sugared strawberries with the lemon juice and a pinch of the salt. Let the mixture stand. Whip the cream until thick. Fold the cream into the strawberry mixture. Beat the egg whites until thick but not dry, gradually adding the remaining sugar. Add to the strawberry mixture. Blend thoroughly. Pour into the chilled graham cracker crust. Refrigerate until firm. Garnish with the sliced strawberries and the whipped cream.

Makes 6 servings.

Elvis on the set of Roustabout.

Blackberry Cobbler

5¼ cups fresh blackberries
¼ cup sugar
Juice from one lemon
2 tablespoons quick-cooking
  tapioca
1½ tablespoons melted butter

1½ cups all-purpose flour
2 teaspoons baking powder
¼ cup packed light brown
  sugar
¼ cup butter, melted
½ cup cream

Grease an 8-inch square baking pan and set it aside.

Wash the berries under cold running water. In a large bowl combine the berries, sugar, tapioca, and lemon juice. Pour the batter into the prepared baking pan. Drizzle melted butter over the top.

In a separate bowl combine the flour, baking powder, brown sugar, and butter. Blend in the cream. Stir until the dough becomes stiff. Spoon on top of the berries. Bake at 425° for 25 minutes or until the crust is golden. Let cool before serving.

Makes 5 servings.

*F*lora Lewis tells of spending her youth pursuing Elvis:

"I first knew him when he lived at the hotel on Wilshire Boulevard. That was when he came back from the army in 1960. I was a student at Hollywood High then, and several of my friends and I went down to the hotel as soon as we got out of school everyday. We just stood around, waiting to see him if he came outside. When he moved to the house in Bel Air, we went there, too.

"If Elvis decided to have a get-together, his friends would come out and pick out a dozen or so people to come up to the house and join them. They really weren't parties at all, at least not in the way most people think of Hollywood parties. It would be just a bunch of people sitting around watching television. There were always lots of snacks—potato chips, cookies, crackers—and soft drinks. There was never any alcohol. It was just that kind of thing, people sitting around talking and eating. The television set was always on.

"Sometimes we would sing while Elvis played the piano. Sometimes we played pool. He was actually pretty quiet most of the time." ■

On the set of **Roustabout.**

Butterscotch Cookies

3½ cups all-purpose flour
1 teaspoon baking powder
½ teaspoon baking soda
1 teaspoon cream of tartar
¼ teaspoon salt
1 cup butter

2 cups packed light brown
  sugar
1 egg, beaten
3 tablespoons evaporated milk
1 teaspoon vanilla extract

Grease a baking sheet and set it aside.

In a medium bowl sift the flour. Remeasure 3½ cups of flour. Resift with the baking powder, baking soda, cream of tartar, and salt. In a large bowl cream the butter with the sugar. Beat until light and fluffy. Add the beaten egg and mix thoroughly. Add the flour mixture a little at a time. If the batter becomes too thick, add the evaporated milk to make it thin. Add the vanilla. Blend thoroughly.

Mold the dough into a roll. Wrap in waxed paper. Refrigerate for 1 day. Cut the dough into slices. Place on the prepared baking sheet. Bake at 400° for 7 minutes.

Makes 4 dozen.

With Hope Lange on the set of Spinout.

Coconut Macaroons

2 cups grated coconut
½ teaspoon grated lemon rind,
packed
1 teaspoon fresh lemon juice

¼ teaspoon salt
½ cup sweetened condensed
milk

Grease a baking sheet and set it aside.

In a medium bowl place the grated coconut. In a separate bowl blend the grated lemon rind, lemon juice, and salt. Add the condensed milk. Pour over the coconut. Toss until the coconut is coated. Drop by teaspoons onto the prepared baking sheet. Shape into mounds. Bake at 325° for 12 minutes or until lightly browned. Immediately remove to a cooling rack.

Makes 18.

Coconut Cookies

3 cups all-purpose flour
3 teaspoons baking powder
¾ teaspoon salt
¾ cup butter
1¼ cups sugar

1½ cups shredded coconut
2 eggs, beaten
1 teaspoon vanilla extract
⅔ cup milk

Grease a baking sheet and set it aside.

In a medium bowl sift the flour. Remeasure 3 cups of flour. Sift again with the baking powder and salt. In a separate bowl cream the butter with the sugar. Beat until light and fluffy. Add the shredded coconut and eggs and blend thoroughly. Add the vanilla. Add to the flour mixture a little at a time alternately with the milk. Refrigerate until the dough is stiff.

Drop by teaspoons onto the prepared pan. Bake at 400° for 8 minutes.

Makes 4 dozen.

Cream Cheese Cookies

1½ cups all-purpose flour
½ teaspoon salt
½ cup butter

3 ounces cream cheese
2 tablespoons sugar
⅛ teaspoon fresh lemon juice

Grease a baking sheet and set it aside.

In a medium bowl sift the flour. Remeasure the 1½ cups of flour. Sift again with the salt. In a separate bowl cream the butter with the cream cheese. Blend until smooth. Add the sugar. Mix until light and fluffy. Add the lemon juice. Add the liquid mixture to the flour mixture.

Roll the dough out on a floured board. Cut with a cookie cutter. Place on the prepared pan. Bake at 350° for 10 minutes.

Makes 4 dozen.

Lemon Cream Cookies

2¼ cups all-purpose flour	1 cup sugar
1 cup butter	2 egg yolks
¼ teaspoon salt	1 teaspoon vanilla extract
3 ounces cream cheese	1 teaspoon grated lemon rind

Grease a baking sheet and set it aside.

In a medium bowl sift the flour. Remeasure 2¼ cups of flour. In a separate bowl cream the butter, salt, and cream cheese until smooth. Add the sugar. Beat in the egg yolks. Mix thoroughly. Add the vanilla and lemon rind. Add the flour a little at a time, mixing well after each addition. Refrigerate the dough for 1 hour.

Roll out ⅓ of the dough at a time on a floured board. Cut with a 2½-inch cutter. Place on the prepared pan. Bake at 400° for 10 minutes or until golden. Remove to cool on a rack.

Makes 3 dozen.

Peanut Butter Cookies

1¼ cups all-purpose flour	½ cup creamy peanut butter
¾ teaspoon baking soda	½ cup sugar
½ teaspoon baking powder	½ cup packed light brown
¼ teaspoon salt	sugar
½ cup butter	1 egg, beaten

Grease and flour a baking sheet and set it aside.

In a medium bowl sift the flour. Remeasure 1¼ cups of flour and sift again with the baking soda, baking powder, and salt. In a separate bowl cream together the butter and peanut butter. Add the sugar and brown sugar. Mix thoroughly. Add the beaten egg. Add the creamed mixture to the flour mixture. Refrigerate until set.

Form the dough into balls 1-inch in diameter. Place on the prepared baking sheet. Flatten with the back of a fork in a crisscross pattern. Bake at 375° for 8 minutes.

Makes 4 dozen.

Pecan Cookies

3 tablespoons butter
1 cup packed light brown sugar
1 egg

1 cup pecan halves
¼ cup all-purpose flour
1 teaspoon vanilla extract

Grease and flour 2 baking sheets and set them aside.

In a saucepan melt the butter. Add the sugar. In a medium bowl beat the egg. Add the pecan halves, flour, and vanilla. Mix thoroughly. Add the melted butter and blend. Drop by teaspoons onto the prepared baking sheets. Bake at 350° for 8 minutes. Let the cookies cool for 1 minute on the baking sheet. Remove to a rack to cool thoroughly.

Makes 3 dozen.

Sour Cream Spice Cookies

3 cups cake flour
1 teaspoon baking soda
1 teaspoon ground cinnamon
½ teaspoon ground nutmeg
½ teaspoon ground cloves
¼ teaspoon salt

⅓ cup butter
2 cups packed light brown
  sugar
2 eggs, beaten
1 teaspoon vanilla extract
⅔ cup sour cream

Grease a baking sheet and set it aside.

In a large bowl sift the cake flour. Remeasure 3 cups of flour. Sift again 3 more times with the baking soda, cinnamon, nutmeg, cloves, and salt. In a large bowl cream the butter with the sugar. Mix thoroughly until light and fluffy. Add the eggs and vanilla. Continue beating until well blended. Add the flour mixture with the sour cream. Mix well. Drop by teaspoons onto the prepared pan. Bake at 350° for 12 minutes.

Makes 3 dozen.

Playing touch football.

*E*lvis's lifestyle in Hollywood was a simple one. He liked watching movies, dating young starlets, and playing touch football at DeNeve Park in Bel Air. Teams consisted of friends Elvis had made while in Hollywood. Included were some of television's leading men and rock 'n' roll stars, including Max Baer, Jr., Kent McCord, Robert Conrad, Gary Lockwood, Ty Hardin, Ricky Nelson, and Dean Torrance. Sometimes Pat Boone joined in the fun. The games continued until residents of the small hilltop enclave requested that Elvis take his football games elsewhere because the crowds of fans were causing unsafe traffic conditions in their community. ■

Chocolate Bars

1 cup melted butter	¼ cup corn syrup
2 cups oats	1½ teaspoons vanilla extract
½ cup packed light brown sugar	6 ounces semisweet chocolate
¼ teaspoon salt	¼ cup chopped walnuts

Grease an 11 x 7-inch baking pan and set it aside.

In a medium bowl blend the melted butter with the oats. Add the brown sugar, salt, corn syrup, and vanilla. Mix thoroughly. Pack the mixture into the prepared pan. Bake at 450° for 10 minutes or until brown. Cool.

In a saucepan melt the semisweet chocolate. Add the chopped walnuts. Remove the bars from the pan. Drizzle the melted chocolate over the top. Refrigerate until the chocolate has hardened. Cut into bars.

Makes 3 dozen.

*I*n 1965 Elvis gave $50,000 to the Motion Picture Relief Fund, and six years later he pledged 2 percent of his salary from one picture to the same fund. This brought his total contribution to the home for failing movie people to $240,000. During this time he was still giving cars as gifts, the way some people buy flowers. ■

Chocolate Creams

2 squares unsweetened chocolate	1 cup chopped walnuts
1⅓ cups sweetened condensed milk	

In the top of a double boiler heat the chocolate with the condensed milk. Mix thoroughly until well blended and the chocolate has melted and become very thick. Cool.

Drop by teaspoons into a bowl of chopped walnuts. Form into balls, coating with walnuts, and place on waxed paper. Refrigerate before serving.

Makes 2 dozen.

Chocolate Caramels

1 cup sugar
1 cup packed light brown sugar
1 cup corn syrup
⅓ cup butter

3 squares unsweetened chocolate
2 cups light cream
1 teaspoon vanilla extract
½ cup chopped walnuts

Butter an 8 x 8-inch baking pan and set it aside.

In a large saucepan blend the sugar, brown sugar, corn syrup, butter, chocolate, and cream. Cook slowly, stirring constantly, until the syrup reaches the soft-ball stage. Remove the pan from the heat. Add the vanilla and walnuts, continuing to stir gently. Pour the mixture into the prepared pan. Cool thoroughly. Turn onto waxed paper and cut into 1-inch squares.

Makes 2 pounds.

Signing autographs on the set of Girls! Girls! Girls!

*D*uring lunchtime at the Paramount commissary, everyone was used to seeing big-name stars like James Cagney, Katharine Hepburn, and Shirley Booth. But when Elvis walked in and ordered a simple lunch, people looked up and took notice. ∎

Strawberry Shortcake

2 cups all-purpose flour
3¾ teaspoons baking powder
½ teaspoon salt
½ cup shortening
¾ cup plus 2 tablespoons milk
3 tablespoons butter, melted

1 tablespoon sugar
Butter, melted
1½ quarts strawberries
Sugar to taste
Cream

Grease a 9-inch cake pan and set it aside.

In a medium bowl sift the flour. Measure 2 cups and resift with the baking powder and salt. Cut in the shortening with a pastry blender. Mix until the dough is crumbly. Add the milk. Mix lightly with a fork. Roll out the dough to ⅓-inch thickness. Place it in the prepared pan. Shape and pat firmly. Brush with the melted butter. Sprinkle the sugar over the top. Bake at 450° for 15 minutes or until the crust is brown.

Split the shortcake while it is still warm. Butter the cut surfaces. Wash the strawberries. Slice them in half. Add sugar to taste and toss lightly. Place half the shortcake on a platter and spoon half of the strawberries on top. Cover with the remaining shortcake. Top with the remaining strawberries and the cream.

Makes 6 servings.

*E*lvis loved to drive through the hills of Bel Air and up and down the Sunset Strip. His Cadillac was custom-made for him by Barris Kustom Industries, 10811 Riverside Drive, in North Hollywood. It was painted with forty coats of diamond and fish scale paint and 24K gold trim. Inside were gold lamé drapes, a well-stocked refrigerator, a hi-fi, and a television. Gold records adorned the ceiling. ∎

Banana Ice Cream

1 pint milk
1 tablespoons all-purpose flour
1 tablespoon water
½ cup sugar
1 egg, separated

1 pint thin cream
½ teaspoon lemon extract
2 bananas
⅛ teaspoon salt

In a saucepan scald the milk, stirring constantly. In a small bowl blend the flour with the water so that the consistency is that of paste. Add the paste slowly to the milk. Cook in the top of a double boiler over hot water for 15 minutes, until the mixture thickens. Add the sugar and beaten egg yolk. Cook for 2 minutes more. Strain through a sieve. When cooled, add the cream and lemon extract.

Peel and scrape the bananas. Push through a sieve. Add with the salt to the milk mixture. Freeze.

Makes 4 servings.

Hot Fudge Sundae

5 squares unsweetened chocolate
1¾ cups sugar
¼ cup light corn syrup
½ teaspoon salt
2 cups boiling water

2 scoops vanilla ice cream
2 teaspoons marshmallow
   cream
2 teaspoons chopped walnuts
Maraschino cherry

In a saucepan melt the chocolate. Cook over low heat for 3 minutes, stirring constantly, until smooth. Add the sugar, corn syrup, and salt. Blend in the water. Continue cooking another 4 minutes. Pour a small amount into a sundae glass just to coat. Add the ice cream. Top with the marshmallow cream, then the chocolate syrup. Sprinkle with the chopped walnuts. Garnish with the maraschino cherry. Store the leftover syrup in the refrigerator.

Makes 1 sundae.

Brown Sugar Shortbread

1 cup unsalted butter	1 teaspoon vanilla extract
1 cup packed light brown sugar	2¼ cups all-purpose flour

Grease a 9-inch cake pan and set it aside.

In a medium bowl cream the butter with the brown sugar and vanilla. Mix until light and fluffy. Add the flour in 4 increments, blending well after each addition. Place the dough in the prepared baking pan. Pat to an even layer. Prick holes in the dough with a fork. Score the dough into evenly-sized wedges. Bake at 325° for 30 minutes or until golden.

Makes 6 servings.

Gingerbread

1¾ cups all-purpose flour	⅛ teaspoon salt
¾ cup sugar	¼ cup butter
¼ tablespoon baking soda	1 egg
¼ tablespoon ground ginger	½ cup molasses
¼ teaspoon cinnamon	½ cup boiling water

Grease and flour a 7 x 11-inch baking pan and set it aside.

In a medium bowl combine the flour, sugar, baking soda, ginger, cinnamon, and salt. Add the butter. Mix until the dough resembles fine crumbs.

In a separate bowl beat the egg. Add the molasses. Slowly add the boiling water. Combine with the flour mixture. Blend until smooth. Pour the batter into the prepared pan. Bake at 350° for 35 minutes.

Makes 8 servings.

Elvis on the set of Girls! Girls! Girls!

Lemon Sherbet

2 teaspoons unflavored gelatin
2 tablespoons cold water
1½ cups sugar
¼ teaspoon salt

2½ cups scalded milk
⅔ cup strained lemon juice
¼ teaspoon grated lemon rind
1 cup whipping cream

Soften the gelatin in the cold water for 5 minutes. In a medium bowl combine the sugar, salt, gelatin mixture, and hot milk. Mix until the gelatin has dissolved and the mixture has cooled. Add the lemon juice and grated rind. Pour the mixture into a freezer tray. Freeze until somewhat mushy. Beat the cream until thick and add it to the sherbet. Freeze until firm.

Makes 8 servings.

Marshmallow Mousse

1 cup milk
6 large marshmallows
1 egg white
¾ cup confectioners' sugar

½ teaspoon vanilla extract
1 pint cream
½ cup chopped walnuts
7 maraschino cherries, halved

In a saucepan heat the milk. Add the marshmallows. Beat until melted. Refrigerate.

In a medium bowl beat the egg white until stiff and fluffy. Add the confectioners' sugar and vanilla. Blend into the marshmallow mixture. Beat the cream until very thick. Add the nuts and maraschino cherries. Add to the marshmallow mixture. Blend thoroughly. Pack the mixture in salt and ice. Freeze for 2½ hours.

Makes 4 servings.

*N*ancy Sharpe began dating Elvis when they met on the set of *Flaming Star*. When the cast and crew went on location in Napa, California, the two were spotted holding hands and stealing kisses over a picnic lunch. ■

Chocolate Custard

2 cups milk
1½ pounds sweet chocolate, broken

6 egg yolks
Whipped cream

In a saucepan add the milk to the broken chocolate. Stir over low heat until the chocolate is melted. Blend until smooth and the mixture begins to boil. Remove the pan from the heat. In a medium bowl beat the egg yolks until well blended. Pour the melted chocolate mixture into the egg yolks and mix thoroughly. Pour into 6 custard cups. Let the custard cool in the refrigerator. Before serving top with whipped cream.

Makes 6 servings.

Elvis and Scatter, his pet chimpanzee.

Banana Pudding

⅓ cup all-purpose flour
¼ teaspoon salt
¾ cup sugar
4 eggs, separated

2 cups milk
½ teaspoon vanilla extract
30 vanilla wafers
6 medium bananas

In the top of a double boiler add the flour and salt to ½ cup of the sugar. Add the egg yolks and milk. Blend thoroughly. Cook over boiling water until thick. Reduce the heat and simmer for 3 minutes. Remove from the heat and add the vanilla.

Pour ⅓ of the custard into the bottom of a casserole dish. Spread evenly. Top with ⅓ of the wafers. Place the sliced bananas on top of the wafers. Continue layering with the custard, wafers, and bananas. Beat the egg whites until stiff and fluffy. Add the remaining sugar. Spread over the pudding. Bake at 425° for 5 minutes.

Makes 6 servings.

Brown Sugar Custard

2 cups milk
1 cup cream
½ cup packed dark brown
   sugar

¼ teaspoon salt
3 eggs, slightly beaten
Chopped walnuts
Shredded coconut

In a saucepan scald the milk and cream. Add the brown sugar and salt. In a medium bowl add the milk mixture slowly to the beaten eggs. Place 5 custard cups into a shallow pan. Fill the pan with hot water to reach almost the tops of the custard cups.

Strain the mixture into the custard cups. Bake at 325° for 30 minutes or until custard tests done. Serve warm. Garnish with the chopped walnuts and shredded coconut.

Makes 5 servings.

*E*d Asner co-starred with Elvis in two films, *Kid Galahad* in 1962 and *Change of Habit* in 1970. Here he tells about working wtih Elvis.

When did you first meet Elvis?
"The first time I met Elvis was when we worked together on the film *Kid Galahad*. I was there about a week. The second film was the same."

Were you nervous about working with Elvis?
"I was so busy in those days working on my own, being sure that I didn't look like a fool. I was concentrating on my own Ps and Qs and at the same time observing, making sure I wasn't setting myself up to look like a fool in front of this great celebrity."

What was your impression of him?
"He was very nice, cooperative. He had a great sense of humor. He generally had a large entourage around him, and they were always clowning or joking. They weren't there to insulate him. They were there because he enjoyed their company."

Any lasting memories of that time?
"I came in with the kind of snobbery you might expect from an actor. What kind of a performance were we going to see from him? After all, this was a remake of a classic. I found him to be straight and direct. My impressions were good. He treated the work with respect, and he was warm and open. He didn't trash anything—himself, the role, the movie, or anybody else. He did not try to act like a superstar. He seemed humble." ■

*W*hen reporters asked Elvis if he knew how to cook, he responded, "I can cook, but nothing that's too fancy. My specialties are frying eggs, bacon, and ham." ∎

Elvis getting a lesson in boxing from trainer Musby Callahan for Kid Galahad.

INDEX